BRUEGEL

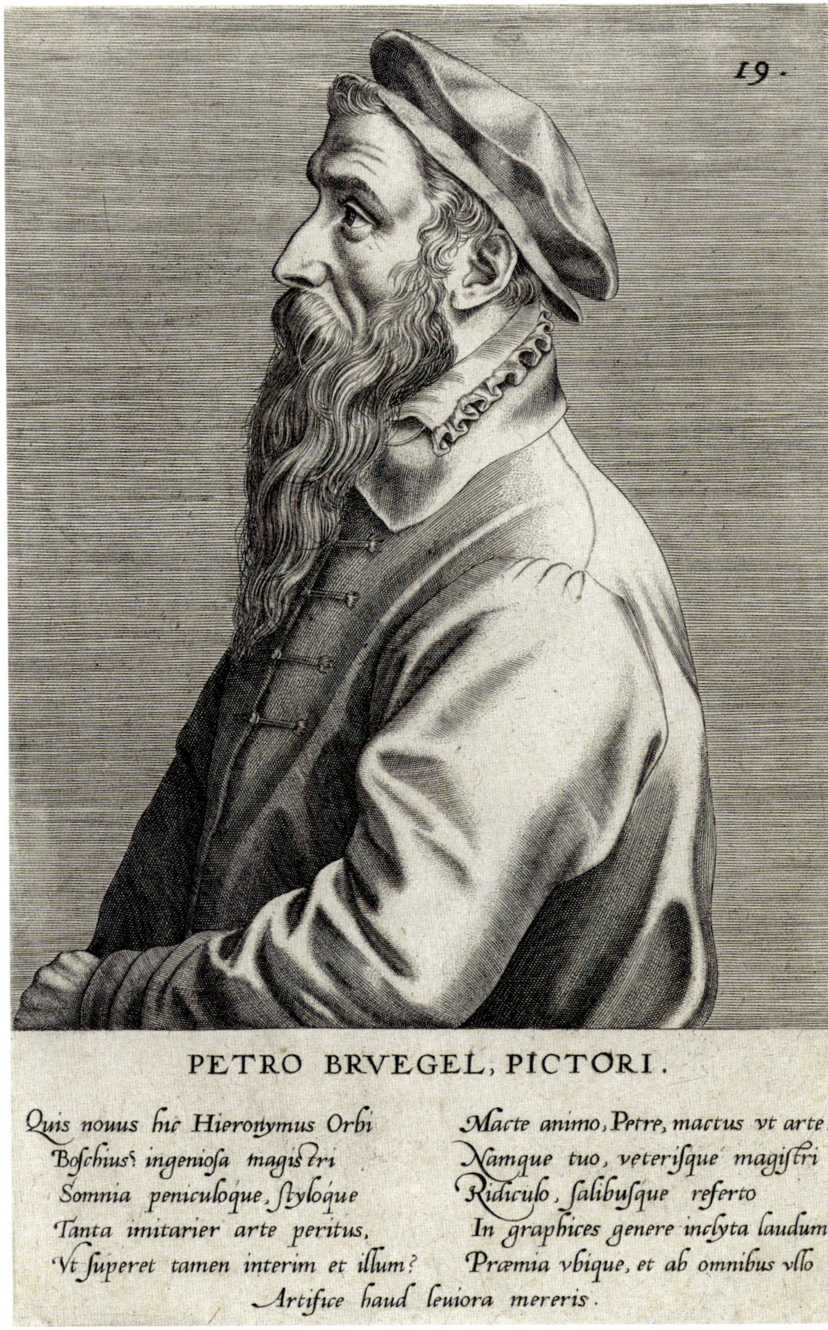

PETRO BRVEGEL, PICTORI.

Quis nouus hic Hieronymus Orbi
Boschius? ingeniosa magistri
Somnia peniculoque, styloque
Tanta imitarier arte peritus,
Vt superet tamen interim et illum?

Macte animo, Petre, mactus vt arte.
Namque tuo, veterisque magistri
Ridiculo, salibusque referto
In graphices genere inclyta laudum
Præmia vbique, et ab omnibus vllo
Artifice haud leuiora mereris.

MASTERS OF ART

BRUEGEL

Florian Heine

PRESTEL
Munich · London · New York

Front Cover: Pieter Bruegel, *Netherlandish Proverbs*, 1559, Staatliche Museen zu Berlin, Gemäldegalerie (detail, see page 51)
Frontispiece: Attributed to Johannes Wierix, *Portrait of Pieter Bruegel the Elder,* 1572, Rijksmuseum, Amsterdam (see page 12)
pages 8/9: *The Fall of the Rebel Angels*, 1562, Musées royaux des Beaux-Arts de Belgique, Brussels (detail, see page 59)
pages 38/39: *The Conversion of Paul*, 1567, Kunsthistorisches Museum, Vienna (detail, see page 97)

A member of Penguin Random House Verlagsgruppe GmbH
Neumarkter Straße 28 · 81673 Munich

1st edition 2026

produktsicherheit@penguinrandomhouse.de

A CIP catalogue record for this book is available from the British Library.

Editorial direction: Anja Besserer
Picture editing: Fiona Krech
Copyediting and proofreading: Vanessa Magson-Mann, So to Speak, Icking
Translation from German: Russell Stockman, Vermont
Production management: Cilly Klotz, Pia Schwarzmann
Design: Florian Frohnholzer, Sofarobotnik
Typesetting: Fotosatz Amann GmbH & Co. KG, Memmingen
Separations: Reproline mediateam
Printing and binding: Livonia Print, Riga
Typeface: Cera Pro
Printed in Latvia
ISBN 978-3-7913-9484-8
www.prestel.com

CONTENTS

INTRODUCTION

Pieter Bruegel the Elder's *The Hunters in the Snow* and *The Peasant Wedding* are among the most popular paintings in art history. The name "Peasant Bruegel", given to the artist in association with these pictures, by no means does justice to the scope of his work. Bruegel was a close observer, a cultured commentator and an intelligent critic of his time, his country and his circumstances. Although he travelled extensively in Italy he failed to adopt the style of the Italian Renaissance then in vogue throughout Europe. He chose a different one. It is astonishing what one does not find in Bruegel. Among the forty-five paintings and roughly sixty-five drawings known to have survived there are no portraits, no nudes, no depictions of deities, no heroicised figures and no idealised bodies. For his art he had no need of them, perhaps because in his own country he had seen and experienced a world that he would not have been able to capture with such a style essentially derived from antiquity.

In the sixteenth century Antwerp, his hometown, became Europe's most important financial centre and a major trading hub. Some fifty percent of the world's trade goods flowed through Antwerp and Rotterdam. Politics takes root where the money is and, along with it in this period, religion.

In 1477, when Holy Roman Emperor Maximilian I married Mary of Burgundy, the Low Countries—which at the time encompassed the present-day Netherlands, Belgium, Luxembourg and a portion of northern France—came under the sway of the Habsburgs. After Maximilian's death in 1519 his grandson Charles V, born in Ghent, was crowned emperor. During Charles's reign an already strong Protestantism spread further throughout Europe. There was no longer only a single Christian truth; thanks to Luther, Calvin, Zwingli and the humanist Erasmus of Rotterdam as well as to the ideas of Sebastian Franck, people could choose different faiths. And because then, as now, religious questions were never solely about religion but also had to do with power, politics and social issues, religion was—and is—exploited.

When Charles's son Philipp II succeeded him on the throne the political-religious situation in the Low Countries, especially for Protestants, became even worse than it had been before. Philipp had been raised a strict Catholic in Spain, had never visited the Low Countries and had no interest in them.

He had not had a humanist education and, like his father, saw as his most important task the promulgation of Catholicism. Open practice of their religion by Protestants was threatened or wholly forbidden; against it Philipp enlisted the powers of the Inquisition, including death by burning, drowning, beheading or hanging, all of which Bruegel and other artists like Frans Hogenberg pictured time and again in their paintings. Moreover, the Low Countries were obliged to pay high taxes to Spain, arousing massive anti-Habsburg sentiment. This combination of economic and religious concerns led to violent opposition and in August 1566 finally culminated in the Great Iconoclasm, in which hundreds of churches and cloisters were plundered and most of their religious artworks destroyed.

Philipp responded not by giving in but by dispatching Fernando Álvarez de Toledo—better known as the Duke of Alba, named governor of the Spanish Netherlands—with a force of several thousand soldiers. Alba, the "Black Legend", instituted a brutal regime. His assignment was to strengthen the royal power and above all punish the rebellious Protestants. For this purpose he convened a special court, the "Council of Troubles" or the "Council of Blood" as it was popularly known. Between 1567 and 1573 the council condemned thousands of people and had them executed by the most horrific of methods, from beheading, breaking on the wheel and hanging to burning at the stake. The previous atrocities were only compounded.

In 1567 Alba's troops plundered Antwerp and Mechelen and burned a number of their buildings; the Spanish governor had thousands of people executed, whether they had been convicted or not. We read in P. C. Hooft's *History of the Netherlands* from 1642 that "the wheels, the stakes, the trees along the roads were laden with strangled, beheaded, martyred corpses, so that people gasped for a breath of air, as if they were now in a common grave, a house of the dead . . .. There was no end to the banishment and expropriation of property".

It is against such a background that one needs to study the Bruegel pictures, far removed from those of the "Peasant Bruegel". Time and again one has to wonder about his religious and political positions. He moved in cultivated and well-to-do social circles, close to the centres of power that he simultaneously criticised. Perhaps he was simply protected by his artistic ability, which was universally admired. But even this question cannot be answered definitively. What makes Bruegel's art still so interesting after nearly 500 years is the universality of its themes and his treatment of them—the way he rendered them on canvas in a fascinating mix of precision and casualness. Bruegel painted many things in his works that one sees only if standing very close to them, which is often difficult. Assistance for seventeen of his works was provided by Vienna's Kunsthistorisches Museum on the occasion of its 2018/19 exhibition *Bruegel, The Hand of the Master*. It created the website www.insidebruegel.net, where one finds not only preliminary drawings and underpaintings in x-ray as well as infrared photographs but also the chance to zoom in on the tiniest details. For anyone who wishes to know more about Bruegel's work the site is a great help and sheer delight.

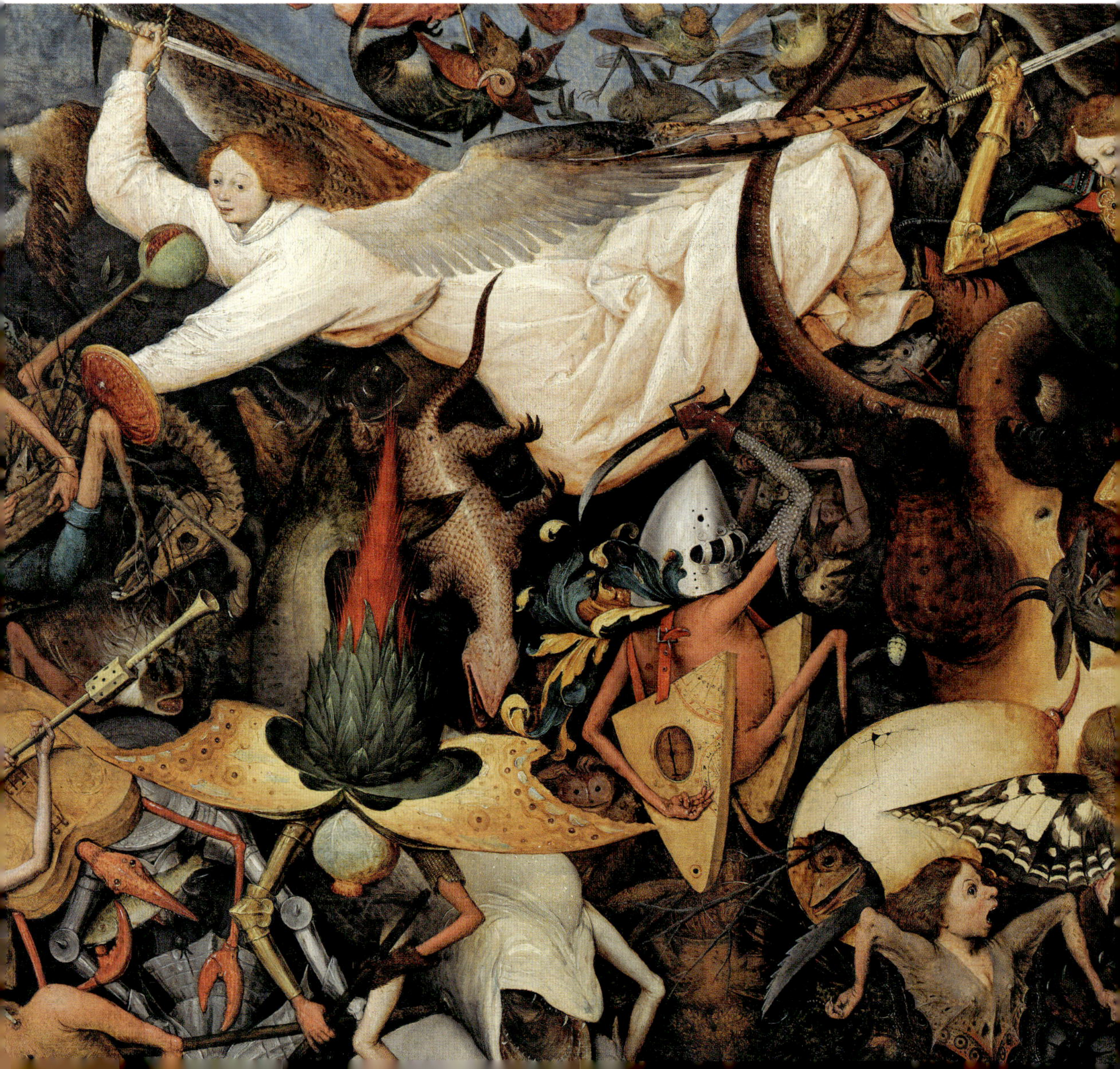

LIFE

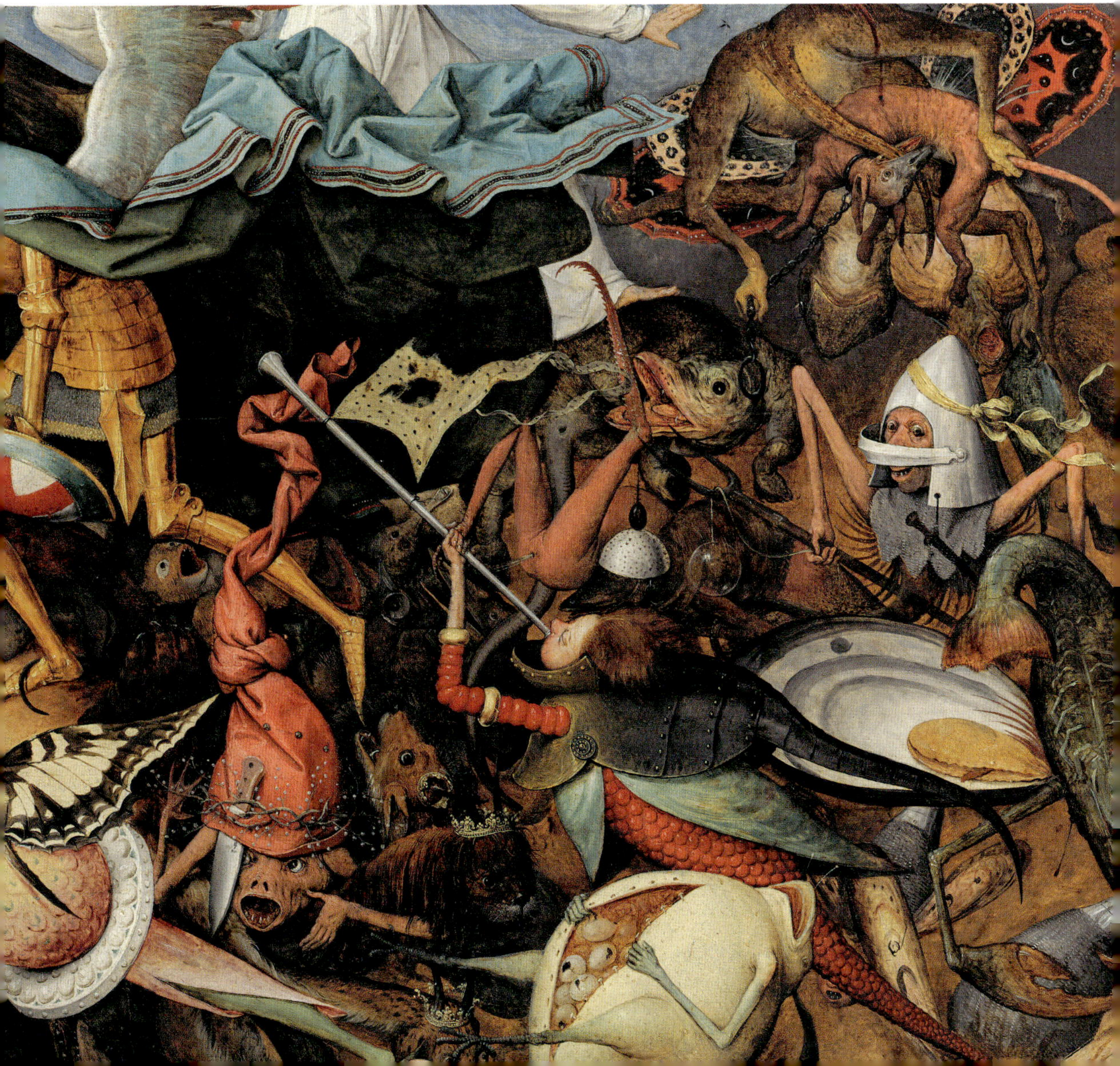

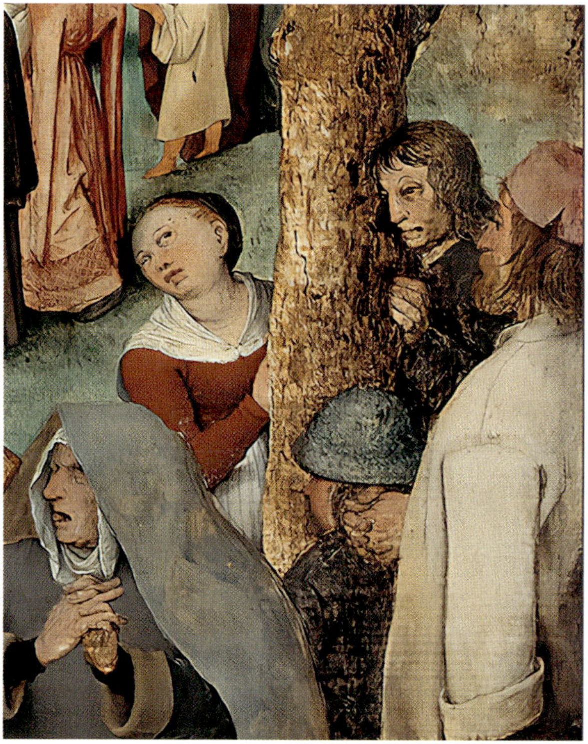

Probable Pieter Bruegel self-portrait in: *The Way to Calvary*, 1564, Kunsthistorisches Museum, Vienna

Pieter Bruegel the Elder

Aside from dated drawings and paintings there are only a few fixed points in Pieter Bruegel's biography. He was born sometime between 1525 and 1530, probably in or near the Dutch city of Breda. We do not know precisely where. The little we do know comes from the pen of Karel van Mander (1548–1606), a painter and writer who in 1604 published his *Schilder-boeck* (*Book of Painters*), a book about the lives of the most important painters since antiquity, virtually a northern version of *The Lives of the Most Excellent Painters, Sculptors, and Architects* by Georgio Vasari (1511–1574), with which the Italian became the "father of art history". The problem with van Mander's narrative is that it appeared thirty-five years after Bruegel's death, twenty-six years after that of his wife and five years after the demise of his mother-in-law. We cannot know how reliable this biography is—but it does provide a few clues. Much the same can be said of his portrait—what did Pieter Bruegel look like? His artist in the famous drawing *The Painter and the Connoisseur* (page 34) is definitely not a self-portrait but it is possible that he did insert himself as a silent observer at the right edges (see detail opposite) of his *The Way to Calvary* (page 77) and *The Sermon of Saint John the Baptist* (page 91). The closest likeness is the one by Dominicus Lampsonius (1532–1599), who as a painter and writer published in 1572 a collection of portraits of Netherlandish artists (*Pictorum aliquot celebrium Germaniae inferioris effigies*) including one of Bruegel (page 12). Although published after Bruegel's death, it is highly probable that the portrait is authentic, for said collection was begun with and during the lifetime of Hieronymus Cock, Bruegel's publisher.

Pieter Bruegel probably received his training in the workshop of the highly versatile painter Pieter Coecke van Aelst (1502–1550). Van Aelst had travelled widely, from 1524 to 1525 in Italy and in 1533 to Constantinople. Produced in his workshop, in addition to large altarpieces, were designs for stained glass and tapestries and even building plans. Moreover, as early as 1539 he was the first to translate into Flemish the *Seven Books on Architecture* (published beginning in 1537) by Sebastiano Serlio (1475–1554), one of the most important architectural treatises of the sixteenth century. A French translation followed in 1545. Van Aelst's wife Mayken Verhulst (c. 1518–1599/1600) was considered one of most important women painters in the Netherlands and was especially successful as a miniaturist. In this complex environment Bruegel seems to have received a very comprehensive introduction to his craft and art.

In 1550 Bruegel helped to produce an altarpiece for the glovers' guild in Mechelen. The main artist was his colleague Pieter Baltens (c. 1527–1584), while Bruegel was responsible for grisaille paintings on the outer wings. The altar, Bruegel's only work commissioned for a church, has not survived. In 1551 the artist was enrolled as a master in the Guild of Saint Luke in Antwerp and from 1552 to 1554 he journeyed by way of France to Italy and then explored the country. It is unclear which cities he visited there and how the young master financed his travels.

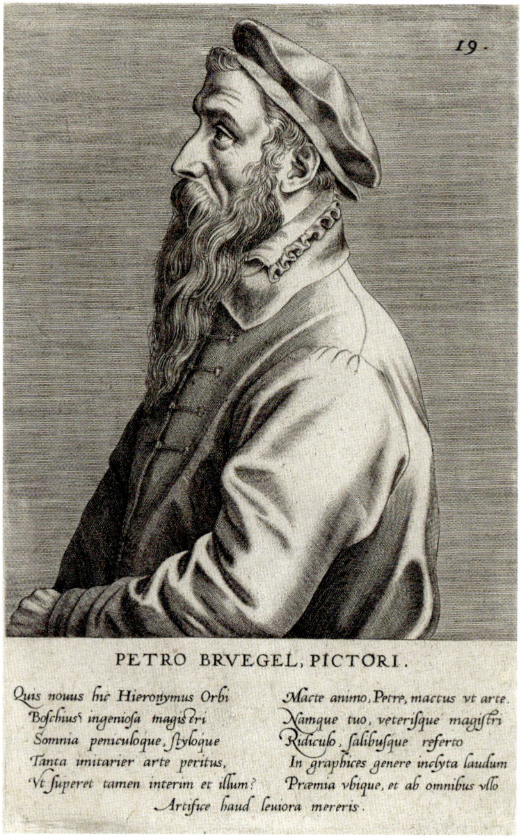

Attributed to Johannes Wierix, *Portrait of Pieter Bruegel the Elder*, 1572, Rijksmuseum, Amsterdam

Bruegel was accompanied on a portion of this journey by his friend and colleague Abraham Ortelius (1527–1598), who later underwent training as a cartographer. In that capacity, in 1579, he published the first modern atlas, the *Theatrum Orbis Terrarum*, which was also a financial success. Their route to Italy probably passed through Dijon, a book publishing and printmaking centre. We know of only selective stops along the way. Bruegel got at least as far as Reggio Calabria and given its proximity to Sicily one would presume that he also crossed the strait. In 1561, long since returned to Antwerp, he produced the drawing for his largest print, the *Naval Battle in the Strait of Messina* (page 13). He subsequently journeyed to Rome by way of Naples where he did a painting of its harbour (now in the Galeria Doria Pamphilj, Rome). In Rome he worked with the very well-known miniature painter Giulio Clovio (1498–1578). There Bruegel drew a peaceful view of the Ripa Grande, Rome's river harbour, which, sadly, has not survived (page 14). From his early drawings his very delicate draughtsmanly style can already be detected: no long, bold lines, only many short strokes and dots with which he was able to create dense, virtuosic landscapes.

We know no more about which cities Bruegel visited in Italy beyond Naples and Rome, whether he saw Florence, Venice or Milan; nor do we know about his actual return route. All that is certain is that the latter led across the Alps. It appears that it was there that he had his most profound experiences of landscape, for the amazing size of the mountain wilderness made a lasting impression on the young painter. Only very few drawings from his journey survive but there must have been hundreds of them, a fund from which he drew for the rest of his life.

It is evident that the Italian sojourn deeply impressed the young artist in terms of landscape but in other artistic respects he remained his own man. Bruegel was definitely inspired by landscape prints from the Italians Domenico Campagnola (1500–1564) and Titian (c. 1488–1576) that were marketed throughout Europe. But unlike most artists who travelled in Italy he did not adopt the

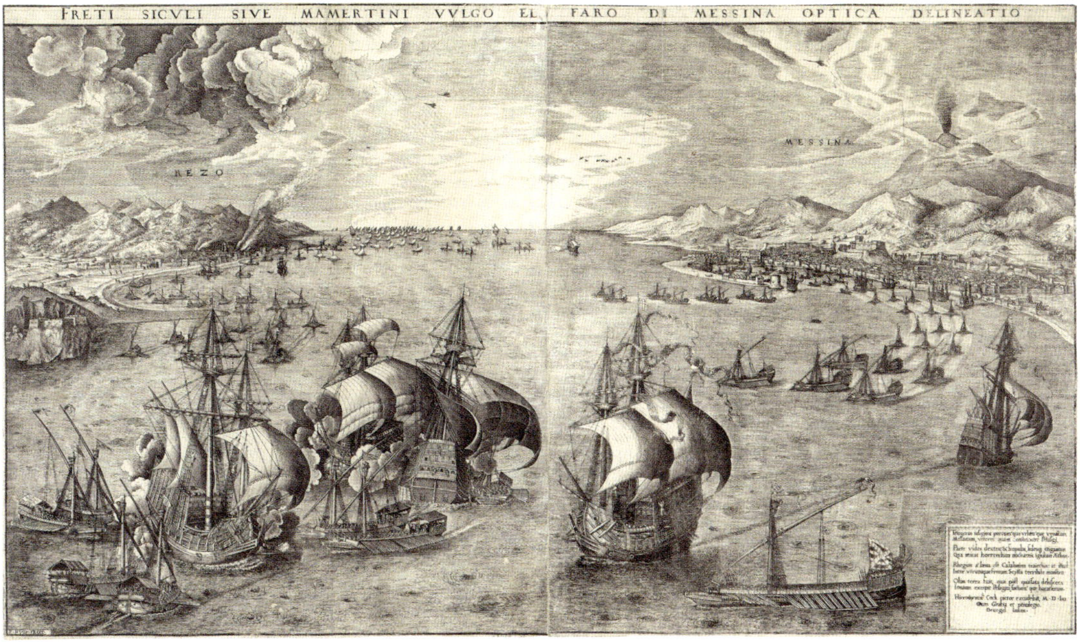

Naval Battle in the Strait of Messina, 1561, Museum Boijmans van Beuningen, Rotterdam

large-figured style; instead, it seems as if Bruegel quite consciously decided against the artistic ideals and standards of the Italian Renaissance. He surely must have seen Michelangelo and Raffael frescoes in the Vatican and possibly works by Titian in Venice, whose treatment of the human form was generally marked by harmony and idealised beauty. He must also have noticed the tricks of perspective to be seen on the ceilings of many of the country's churches. But all this apparently played no major role in the Netherlander's work. Ability is one thing—and he had certainly mastered every technique—but application another. Bruegel simply chose a different path, one more rooted in the art of earlier Dutch painters like Rogier van der Weyden, Jan van Eyck and of course Hieronymus Bosch. Yet aside from the concept of bodies and their movement in space, what actually united artists north and south was their anthropocentric worldview, in which the human being is predominant, whether in larger figures as in the Italians or simply in larger numbers as in Bruegel. He interpreted the Italian Renaissance in a different way, gave it another artistic form for his own purposes and exploited its possibilities by his own means.

What appears to have made a lasting impression on him in addition to the magnificence of the mountains was the insignificance of humankind compared to the vastness of the Alps. An experience he doubtless wanted to convey to his fellow flatlanders (page 15).

Back from his long journey, sometime in the year 1554, Bruegel began his career as a draughtsman and designer of patterns for engravings. What else he did, whether he already set up a painting studio as well, is as unknown as so much else. It is certain that he drew landscapes, for in 1556 his series

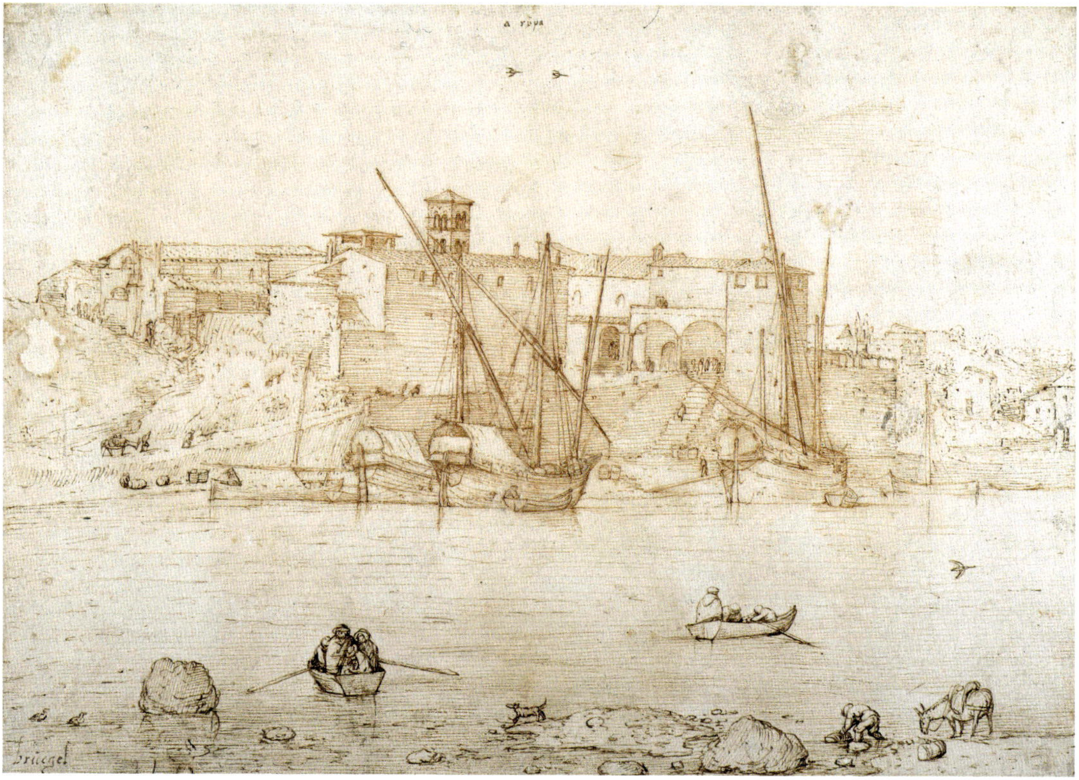

View of the Ripa Grande, 1552/53, Chatsworth House, Bakewell

Large Landscapes was published by Hieronymus Cock (1518–1570). A painter and engraver himself, Cock became the most important publisher of prints in the second half of the sixteenth century. He was known for his series *Praecipua monimenta*, twenty-six landscapes depicting ruins in the city of Rome that he drew and engraved himself. At that time Rome was once again becoming the cosmopolitan city it had been in antiquity—this time not under the dominion and guidance of heathen emperors but rather Christian popes, who in their conduct were scarcely distinguished from their ancient predecessors. Cock issued this series of prints in his publishing company Aux Quatre Vents which was founded in 1548. He published not only his own works but also those of many colleagues such as Maarten van Heemskerck (1498–1574), who painted imposing views of the construction of Saint Peter's Basilica. The company's range was extensive, offering roughly a thousand different prints for sale, from landscapes and architecture to city views, portraits and satires. Its choice of artists was also varied. In addition to those already mentioned there was Frans Floris (1516–1570), an "Italianist" and decided proponent of the Italian concept of Renaissance painting, which is unsurprising when one learns that he and his brother had studied in Rome. But the house also published works by Frans

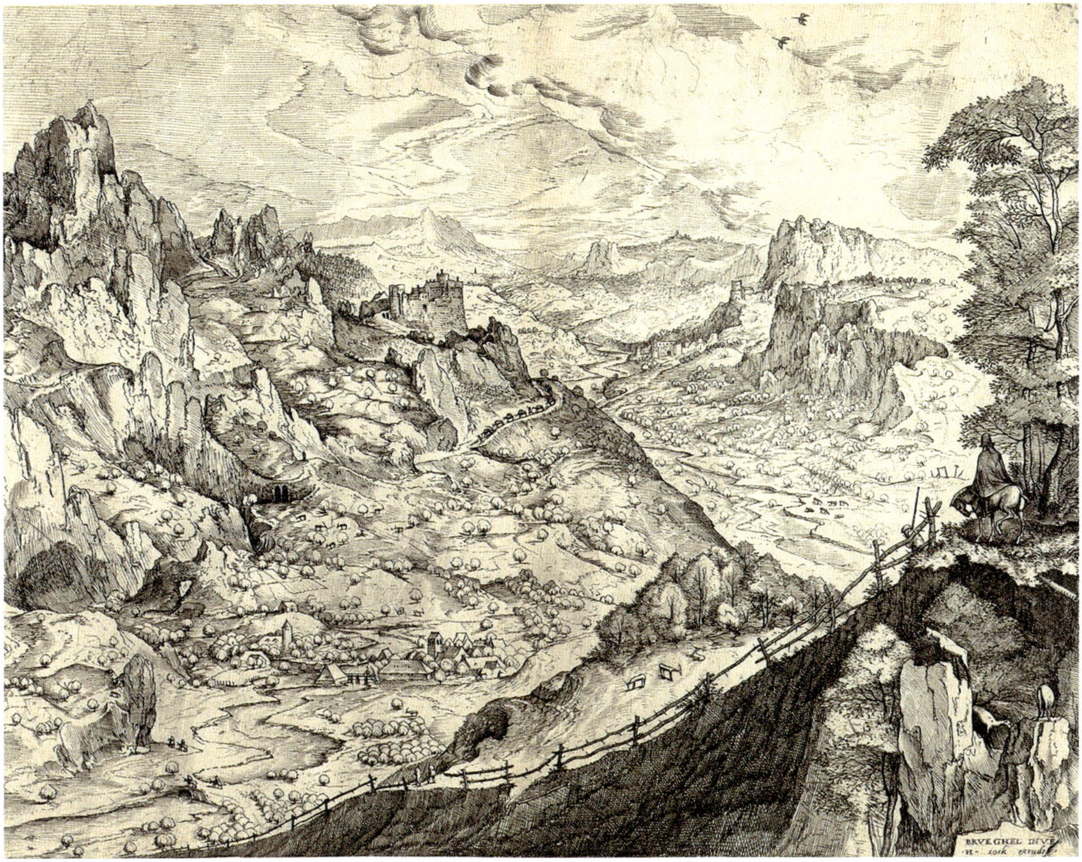

Large Alpine Landscape, c. 1555–1557, Staatsgalerie Stuttgart

Hogenberg (1535–1590), who drew and engraved satires and city views.

It is conceivable that Bruegel had contact with Hieronymus Cock even before his journey. Perhaps Cock had noticed Bruegel's extraordinary draughtsmanly talent and helped finance the Italian journey in the hope of publishing the up-and-coming artist's drawings after his return. For after that return and up to the time of his death Bruegel did in fact work for and with Cock and Aux Quatre Vents. His twelve-sheet *Large Landscapes*, issued there in 1556, has no clear theme aside from landscape and no inner cohesiveness other than the size of the prints. Many of the views feature everyday subjects like farm work, others religious ones like the *Landscape with the Flight into Egypt*, and still others took on their meaning only during the process of their creation. *The Road to Emmaus* (pages 16/17) is one such example: in his sketch Bruegel characteristically pictured three hikers descending into a hamlet as repoussoir figures between two trees. In the print only one tiny detail

The Road to Emmaus, 1555/56,
The Metropolitan Museum of Art, New York

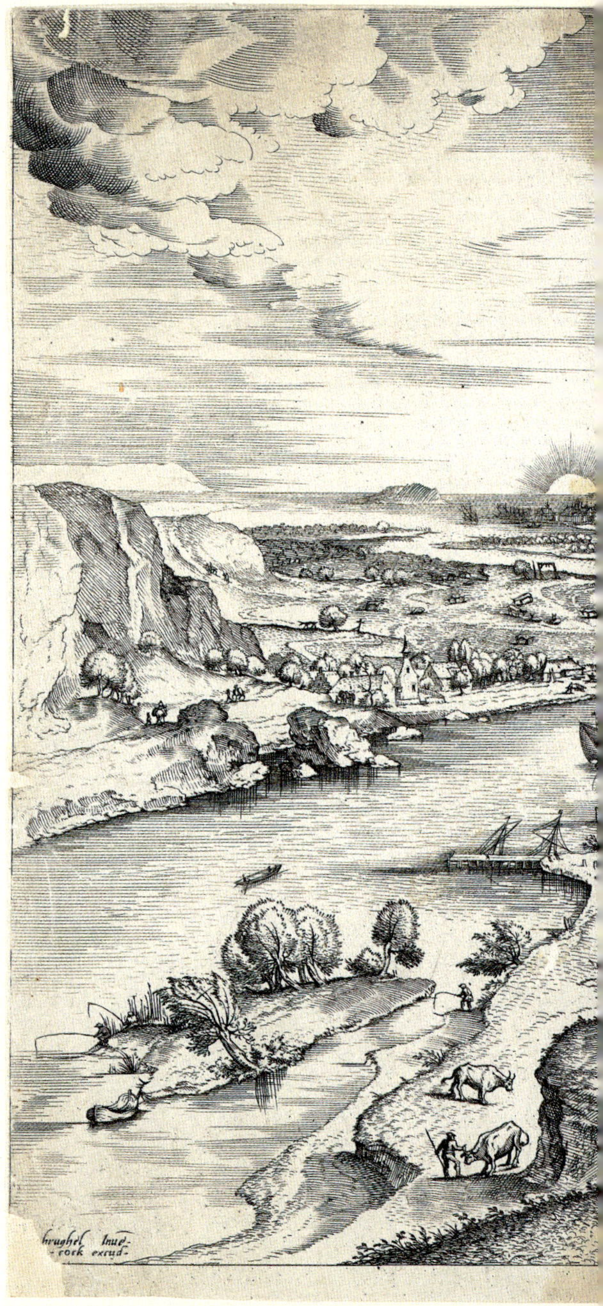

has been changed, one that nevertheless turned a simple landscape with hikers into the biblical narrative identified in the picture title: *Euntes in Emmaus* (*The Road to Emmaus*). In the print the middle hiker has been given a filigree halo, which makes of the three figures two apostles on their way to Emmaus who have been joined by Jesus, whom they recognise only when he breaks bread with them in the evening (Luke 24:13–35). It is unclear who had the idea of "enriching" the content, whether the artist, the engraver, or the publisher, but it was most probably the last named, for it was up to him to decide how a print was to look and how it was to be titled.

We do not know how many and what drawings Bruegel made during his long stay in Italy. For his series, however (with the exception of *Tivoli*), he did not use any recognisable vedute but rather composed new landscapes, employing a method he applied in many of his paintings and that became typical of his style. From an elevated standpoint one looks down onto a picture plane in the near foreground on which trees and people appear as repoussoir figures. They lead the viewer's gaze into a broad middle ground flanked by hills and mountains and into the picture's depth, where a river meanders before passing through a village or a city and emptying into the ocean, which finally forms the horizon. These landscape compositions are structured with diagonals that produce different planes and with trees in the foreground that generally take up the entire height of the picture as vertical accents. What is fascinating about this is Bruegel's holistic conception, his rendering of

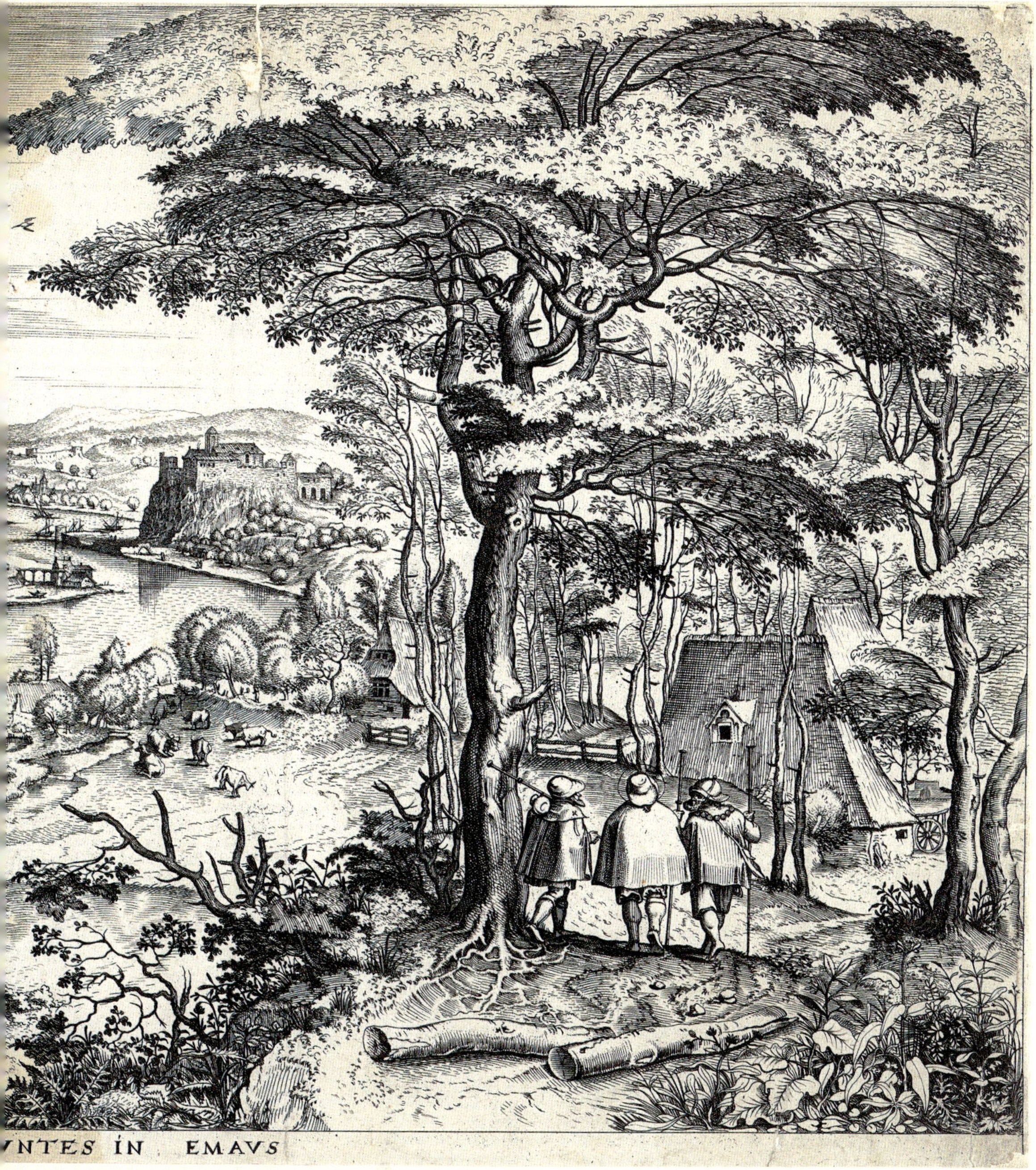
VNTES IN EMAVS

the complete picture space from the foreground to the farthest distance. Trees, ships, buildings, hills and people appear smaller the farther away they are. One notes that Bruegel had perfected his perspective, possibly in Italy, and interpreted it for his own artistic purposes. His pictures do not centre on a single individual but on humankind as such, embedded in grandiose nature.

Whether this natural landscape is one he had seen in Italy and sketched on the spot or an imaginary composition based on his drawings is ultimately immaterial. What matters is its effect. In his *Schilderboeck* Karel van Mander expressed it somewhat drastically: "On his journeys he drew many views from nature, so it is said that he swallowed mountains and cliffs when he was in the Alps and back home spat them out again onto canvases and wooden panels". Not a pleasant image, but an explanation of why it is impossible to assign any of his landscapes to actual places.

The series was engraved by the experienced brothers Joannes (1530–1605) and Lucas (died c. 1590) van Doetecum. All in all such a series was an expensive undertaking. How much Cock paid is unknown but we do know what his colleague Christoph Plantin (1520–1589) paid for a book he published and so Cock probably went to a similar expense. The draughtsman received 3.5 gulden for his design. A craftsman's average monthly pay at the time was around 6.5 gulden. For his very time-consuming work the engraver, in turn, earned roughly twice as much as the draughtsman. The financial risk lay with the publisher, for he not only had to correctly assess the public's taste but also which artists were best suited for which project. There are no longer any indications of print runs, but it is assumed that costs like honoraria for designers and engravers and material costs (paper, ink, printing machines etc.) were covered if 300 prints were sold. Editions of 1,000 to 1,500 were by no means unusual. Often even more prints were made from a single plate that needed retouching after wear.

For the young Bruegel this collaboration not only meant an income but also the chance to gain experience and become internationally known. How successful such undertakings could be is clear from the example of Albrecht Dürer, who thanks to his prints marketed throughout Europe, was already a celebrity in the Netherlands before he spent a year there in 1520/21 and was accordingly received as such. Bruegel enjoyed similar success: in the second edition of his *Lives* from 1568 Vasari included Bruegel. Since he had never been in the Netherlands and had not seen any of the artist's paintings, his knowledge is certain to have come from prints marketed in Italy. For the young artist this was a way to make a name for himself. Paintings took a lot of time and were costly to produce, so a painter needed a well-to-do patron—hard enough for an unknown artist to find still today.

Virtue and Vice

Among Bruegel's early successful prints were *The Temptation of Saint Anthony* (page 41) from around 1556 and *Big Fish Eat Little Fish* from 1557 (page 43), both of which borrowed stylistic elements from Hieronymus Bosch. And that's not all: whereas no draughtsman is named on the Anthony print and it could be assumed that the design originated with the great master, on the *Fish* print it is actually Bosch's name that appears, not Bruegel's. This was purely for commercial reasons; Bosch drawings were still much sought after and it was the publisher's decision to market Bruegel's works this way. Strange as this might seem today in the long run the deception was useful, as by doing so Cock launched Bruegel as a "legitimate" successor of Bosch. In later editions actually credited to Bruegel there is no qualitative difference between the supposed work of Bosch and that of the legitimate successor, since both came from the same hand. In the following *Vices* series Bruegel is named as the draughtsman. This was obviously effective on the international market, for in Ludovico Guicciardini's *History of the Netherlands* from 1567 the Italian writes: " . . . Pieter Bruegel from Breda, a great imitator of the science and fantasies of H. Bosch, for which reason he came to be known as the second Hieronymus Bosch." Guicciardini had written the book as early as 1560, long before its actual publication, so he was unaware of the Bruegel works that no longer had anything to do with Bosch.

There were plenty of Bosch successors as it was, for he represented an important element of Netherlandisch painting. Joachim Patinir (c. 1475–1524), Jan Mandyn (c. 1500–c. 1559), Pieter Huys (c. 1520–c. 1581), Herri met de Bles (c. 1510–c. 1550–55) and Jan Wellens de Cock (1490–1528), the brother of the publisher, followed in that pictorial tradition. That Bruegel stood out among the many Bosch successors, even internationally, was owing to the publisher's marketing of prints that now bore his name. They were sold all over Europe, the publishing house Aux Quatre Vents was, after all, the market leader.

The essential difference between Bosch and Bruegel's monsters lies in their supposed provenance. To Bosch's thinking evil was the spawn of hell and the devil which manifested itself in such monsters. For Bruegel, however, sins, vices and evil in general were not necessarily rooted in hell or the devil but in humankind itself; they were simply human qualities. For Bosch evil came from Satan, and humankind was caught up in the battle between heaven and hell; for Bruegel, by contrast, evil was a part of being human. He exposes it as something created by people, for evil is often simply a choice and its execution, something willed.

From 1557 to 1560 Bruegel drew two new series of prints that were again published by Cock. This time the engraver was Pieter van der Heyden (c. 1530–after 1572). The first series presented vices, or, as they are often called, the Seven Deadly Sins. It includes *Pride* (*Superbia*, page 45), *Avarice* (*Avaritia*), *Lechery* (*Luxuria*, page 21), *Envy* (*Invidia*), *Gluttony* (*Gula*), *Indolence* (*Accidia*) and *Wrath* (*Ira*). In the Middle Ages these vices were widely illustrated in illuminated books and wall paintings and appeared as sculpture programmes on church portals. Bruegel still signed this series with the name Brueghel, which he later changed. It is not known why, perhaps because of the international distribution of his art, in which the "h" was troublesome. More important was the fact that his name appeared on the prints at all.

At this time the vices provided a good opportunity to surprise viewers with a mixture of horror and fascination. From the very beginning the satiric element played an important role as well, as it had with prints, which had not been around for very long yet. Irony and satire generally sold well, as is evident with Sebastian Brant's *Ship of Fools* from 1494, which became a European bestseller.

In this series Bruegel again plunged into the world of Hieronymus Bosch; fantastic creatures, bizarre structures, strange weapons, giants and dwarfs, all in illustration of sinful vices. The prints have explanatory subtitles in Flemish as well as Latin for the international public. Unlike his predecessors, Bruegel did not reduce the personifications of sins to statue-like, uninvolved figures, but engaged them in crowded scenes: Gluttony, for example, is guzzling from a tankard, the naked Lechery (Luxuria) cuddles with some sort of canine hybrid (page 21) and Pride (Superbia) appears to be the mistress of her realm (page 45).

After this cycle Bruegel seems to have finally put Bosch's legacy behind him, at least as far as printmaking was concerned. Time and again there would be fantastic, twisted figures in certain prints but they were no longer quotes from Bosch but from Bruegel himself.

In 1559 Bruegel began the series on the counterparts of the *Vices*, the *Virtues*, among them *Charity* (*Caritas*), *Justice* (*Justitia*), *Faith* (*Fides*), *Hope* (*Spes*), *Prudence* (*Prudentia*), *Moderation* (*Temperantia*) and *Strength* (*Fortitudo*). They too stand in a long tradition in which allegorical figures are seen grouped around a central female figure, generally labelled as an allegory of the given virtue. Bruegel now created something new on various levels. His allegories stand in the centre of the picture to be sure, with the appropriate attribute on their heads, but they seem to be wholly uninvolved in what is taking place around them. And there was a lot going on, for this was Bruegel's other invention: he presents realistic scenes from the "real" life of his time. And does so in a special way, as he indeed illustrates the (theoretical) virtues, but only a single facet of them: for example, in *Justice* (page 47) we see only punitive justice, not grace or forgiveness. Bruegel turns our expectations inside out. Hope stands on an anchor in the water (!) at such a forsaken post that the viewer has to wonder what sort of hope one can cling to. In *Strength* only military might and brutality are apparent, nothing of an inner strength coming from the heart that can also do good. These scenes are not theoretical and divorced from reality; in realistic settings they illustrate a potential discrepancy between the theory and practice of the given virtues, which in the artist's interpretations degenerate into vices and deadly sins. The only difference appears in

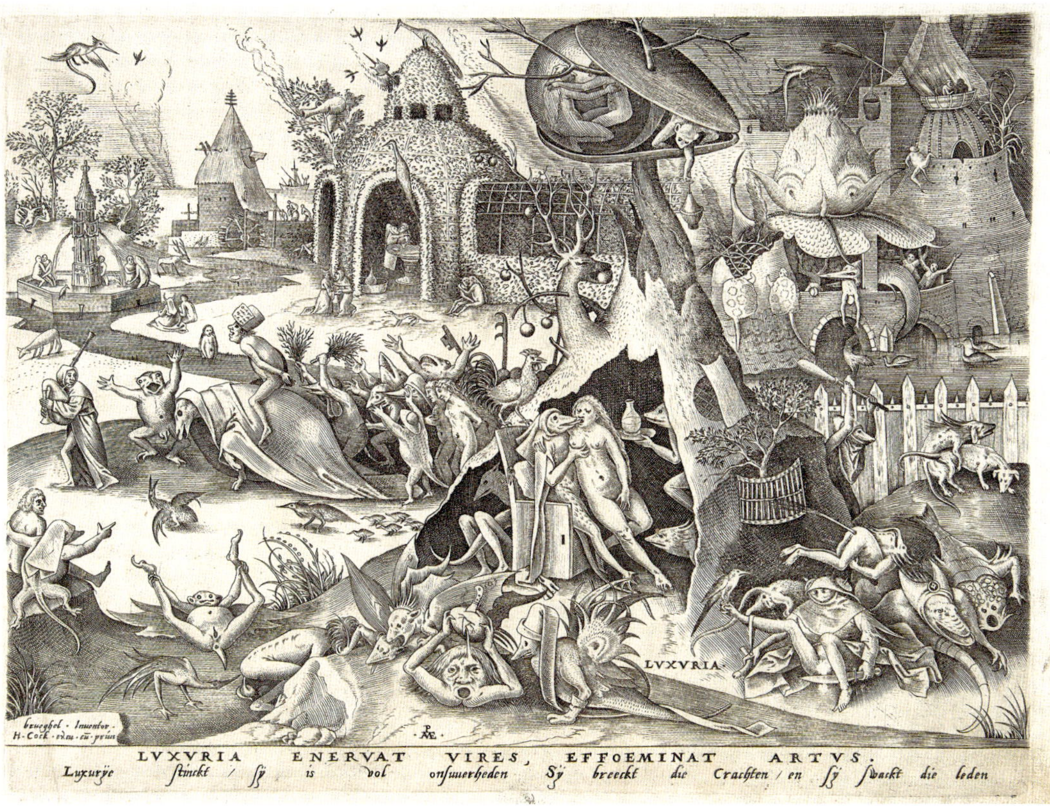

Lust (Luxuria), 1558, The Metropolitan Museum of Art, New York

Moderation (*Temperantia*) (page 22), where the allegory has a bridle in her mouth and wears a clock on her head as a symbol of time's passing. The tie between moderation and the seven liberal arts (grammar, dialectic, geometry, astronomy, music, rhetoric [theatre] and arithmetic) follows a textual tradition since antiquity. In Seneca the application of the virtues (above all moderation) to the liberal arts was already considered the path to wisdom, a belief continued in medieval writing. Bruegel was the first to establish this connection in a picture. And here it becomes clear why the personifications are always female: this shows that they are not specific people but allegories, for traditionally women had no access to the liberal arts. Thus the figures represent the concept, not the woman herself. In his picture the painter and draughtsman Bruegel adds sculpture, architecture and, at the far left, painting as active protagonists, even though they did not number among the liberal arts but rather were part of the *artes mechanicae* or craftsmanship. But in Renaissance times this changed; the fine arts were elevated from craft status to the liberal arts, hence Bruegel's inclusion of them. One astonishing artistic touch is the globe in the picture's background, on which

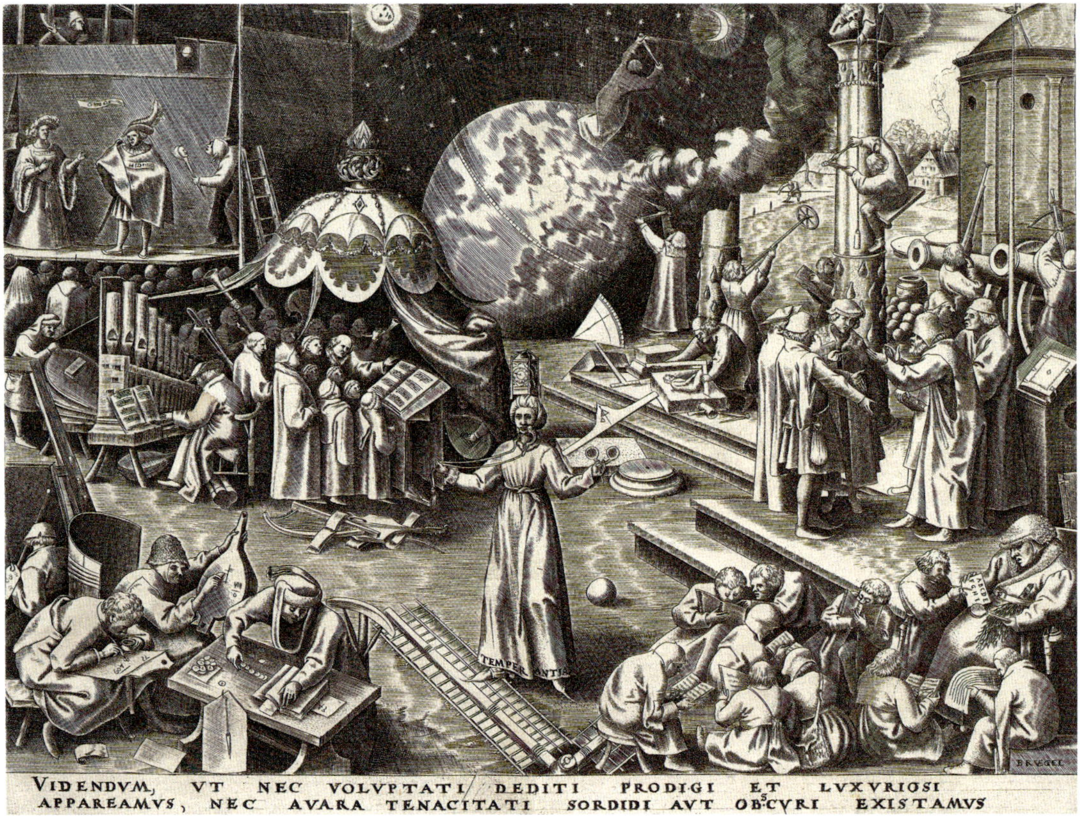

Moderation (Temperantia), 1559/60, The Metropolitan Museum of Art, New York

an astronomer is attempting to measure his distance from the moon with a compass. And he is apparently doing so on a rotating terrestrial globe accompanied by little lines that show it to be spinning very fast. This is the first time an artist created the illusion of speed in such a way.

In all the prints of the series the allegorical figures, unlike the Vices, stand in the centre of the picture as if they have—and indeed do not want to have—nothing to do with the actions taking place in their names. Bruegel is contemplating important ethical questions here, not abstractly but in relation to real life. He deals with morality in a social context and in the Netherlands of Pieter Bruegel this was turbulent indeed (see introduction).

He Begins to Paint

With the publication of his prints of landscapes, virtues and vices Bruegel had achieved an artistic reputation and he now devoted himself increasingly to painting. His first work is thought to have been *Landscape with the Parable of the Sower* (page 24), which is dated 1557. Here much of what Bruegel had already presented in his landscape prints and would continue to deploy in his following paintings can be appreciated. This does not mean that he abandoned printmaking; on the contrary: between 1561 and 1565 a series of ship pictures was issued (page 57) that he had drawn and published with Cock. Time and again Bruegel prints were published by Cock's company, including the posthumous *The Battle of the Moneybags and Strongboxes* (page 109).

His early works, like the famous so-called "busy pictures" (pages 51, 53) are more similar in their arrangement to his drawings than to his later paintings. As Erasmus von Rotterdam (c. 1467–1536) had collected proverbs and idioms in his *Adagia* (published in 1500, expanded in 1508, 1533), Bruegel also did so (page 51), but as pictures depicting the proverbs, Carnival customs and children's games (page 25), which he executed with remarkable meticulousness, love of detail and a certain wink of the eye. Here again he employed his compositional principle of the panoramic overview; this allowed him to include a full 119 proverbs and roughly 90 games in their respective paintings. For such works, which cost him a great deal of time and material expense, he needed suitable patrons. We do not know who commissioned him to paint his busy pictures or whether they were his own idea. The same is true of his busy picture of horror, *The Triumph of Death*—a farewell to hope—which he painted in 1562/63 (page 61). Who would have commissioned such a work? What sort of circles did Bruegel move in?

The artist doubtless had excellent connections in elite and intellectual circles in Antwerp, Brussels and Mechelen. As in contrast to the fostered cliché of the "Peasant Bruegel" who had grown up and been more or less educated in the country and for that reason was able to portray rustics with all of their mannerisms—van Mander writes that he was "born among peasants, . . . thanks to which he could capture peasants with his brush", Bruegel was in fact more of a city dweller and certainly had a solid education and a correspondingly cultured background. His prints already attest to a remarkable gift for observation and conceptualisation shaped by profound philosophical and political thinking. So who belonged to his urban circle? First of all Abraham Ortelius, with whom he travelled in Italy and who in turn had close ties to Christoph Plantin, one of the most important printers and publishers of his time. His publishing house issued more than a thousand books during his lifetime, from the first multilingual Bible to Ortelius's first atlas. Although he was forced to flee to Paris for a year for having published "heretical" writings and was the official printer for the Protestant Netherlandish General States, Plantin was awarded the printing monopoly of all the liturgical books for Spain and the Spanish Netherlands and their colo-

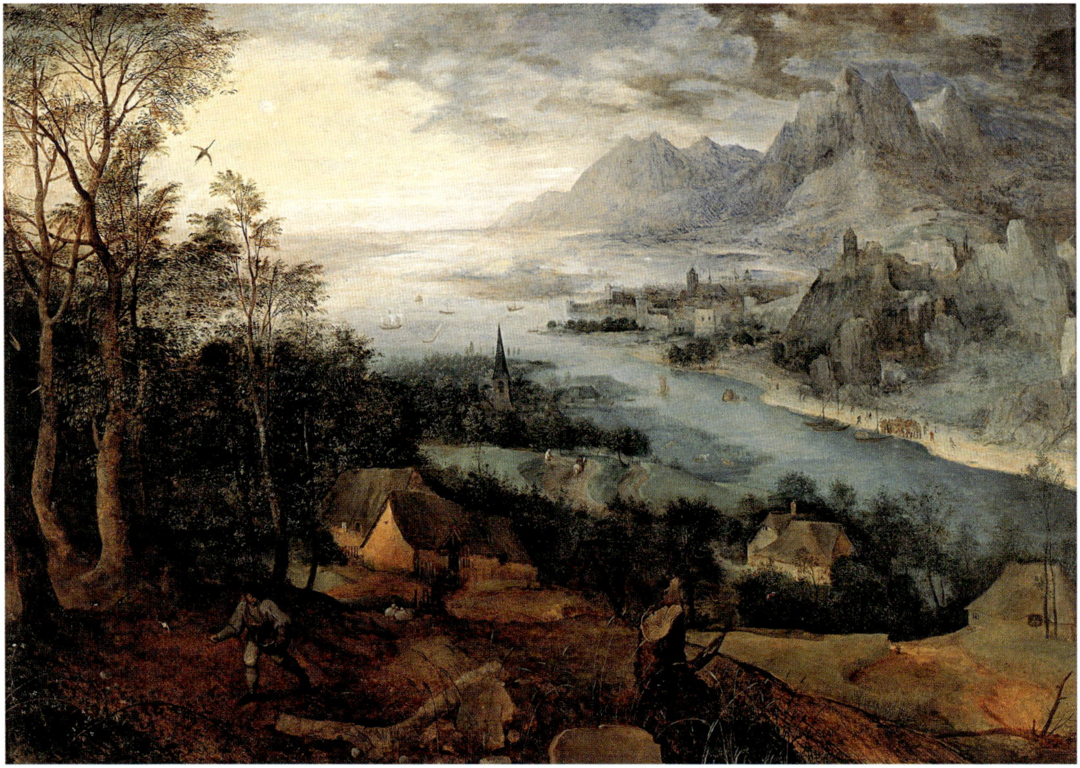

Landscape with the Parable of the Sower, 1557, Timken Museum of Art, San Diego

nies by the Catholic King Philipp II. Among other things he also published works by Erasmus of Rotterdam and Sebastian Franck (1499–1542). Their writings were widely distributed and influential in the Netherlands, though many Catholics considered them to be heretical. Erasmus questioned the institution of the Church with its rituals and sacraments and called for an inner experience of God. Franck was more of a religious philosopher who also railed against the Church as the root of all evil. For him as well, the union of Church and state was a betrayal of Christian teaching. In his *Paradoxa* from 1534 he argued for a non-denominational stance and called for an "invisible Church", a "Church of the heart", as well as for amicable relations between confessions. Since God revealed himself in all religions, He could not be appropriated by one or another. Such ideas could not have been welcomed by the Spanish inquisitorial authorities or even by many Protestants but quite obviously shaped or at least influenced the religious beliefs of Bruegel's circle and the artist himself. Ortelius, for example, recommended the *Paradoxa* as an important theological text in a letter to his nephew.

In 1563 Bruegel married Mayken Coecke (1545–1578), the daughter of his teachers the van Aelsts, after they had all moved to Brussels. The wedding took place in the church Notre-Dame de la Chapelle in which Bruegel was later interred. His son Pieter the Younger was born in 1564 (died

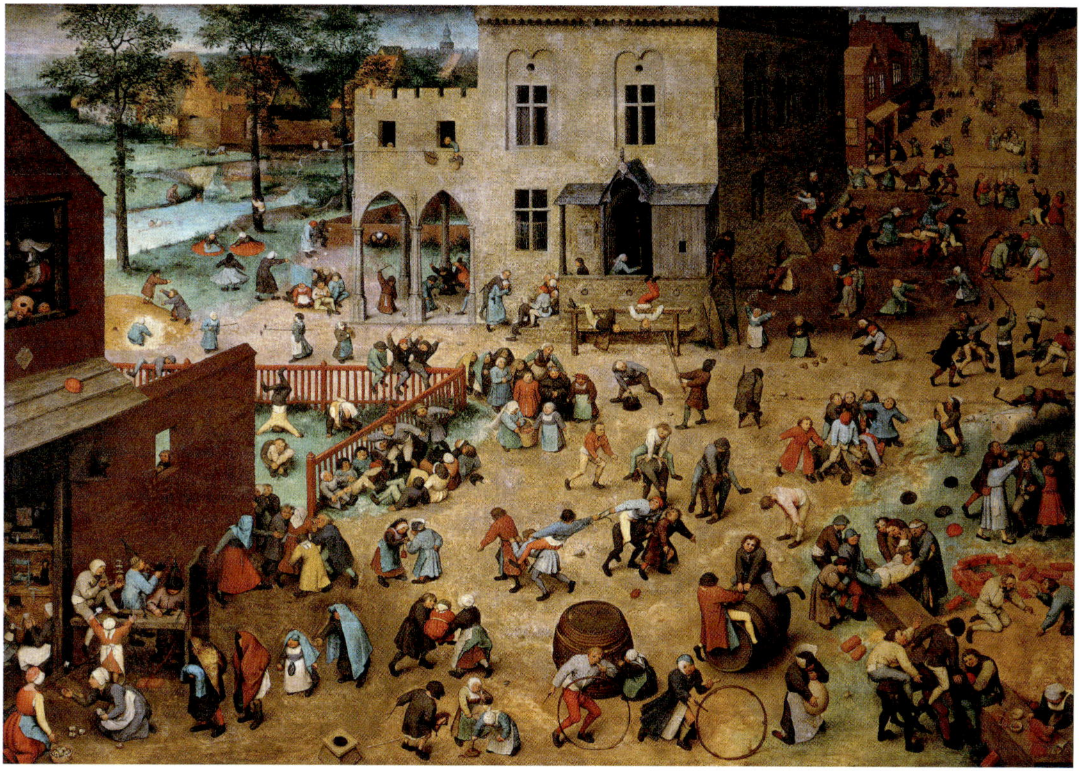

Children's Games, 1560, Kunsthistorisches Museum, Vienna

1638), his daughter Maria in 1566, about whom nothing is known and in 1568 his second son, Jan, who died in 1625.

Also part of Bruegel's circle was Antoine Perrenot de Granvelle (1517–1586), a member of Philipp II's council of state, minister to Margaret of Parma and archbishop of Mechelen. Bruegel got to know him at the latest after his move to Brussels in 1563. Granvelle commissioned Bruegel's *Landscape with the Flight into Egypt* (page 27) and probably owned other works of his as well. The contact had almost certainly been made through the Jongelinck brothers. Jacques (1530–1606), of whom it is also said that for a time at least he travelled with Bruegel through Italy, was a sculptor, medallist and brother of Niclaes Jongelinck (1517–1570), probably Bruegel's most important collector. Niclaes was a tax official and banker and, in addition to works by Frans Floris and Albrecht Dürer, owned at least sixteen Bruegel paintings, including the 1563 *The Tower of Babel* (page 69), *The Way to Calvary* (page 77) and the six paintings of the famous cycle of the seasons, of which only five survive. Which other Bruegel works he owned is unknown.

The Cycle of the Months

Bruegel's acquaintances were thus greatly varied, financially secure and extremely influential politically. It is possible that his contact with Cardinal Granvelle especially, who was considered very liberal for conditions at the time, helped to ensure that Bruegel did not get into trouble with his pictures and that he held a protective hand over him. This is only speculation, of course, but it is not unthinkable.

The Cycle of the Seasons or more correctly the Cycle of the Months commissioned by Jongelinck and painted in 1565 is a high point in landscape painting. At that time painted landscapes were still relatively uncommon, especially in this size. We know of Albrecht Dürer's stops on his Italian journey of 1494 from his watercolours, but the first real, portrait-like landscape paintings were produced by Albrecht Altdorfer in around 1520–25 (*Danube Landscape with Castle Wörth*, Alte Pinakothek, Munich). The two were pioneers of landscape painting. People were not yet accustomed to seeing such pictures, especially since most people knew little more than their own native landscapes. When Dürer sojourned in the Netherlands for a year in 1520/21 he became acquainted with Joachim Patinir, who painted so-called world landscapes. He produced vast landscape panoramas out of all the accustomed elements: hills, mountains and valleys, forests, villages and cities, along with rivers and seas. Into them he inserted mythological or Christian narratives. Bruegel had already drawn from them in his prints and he now did so in his

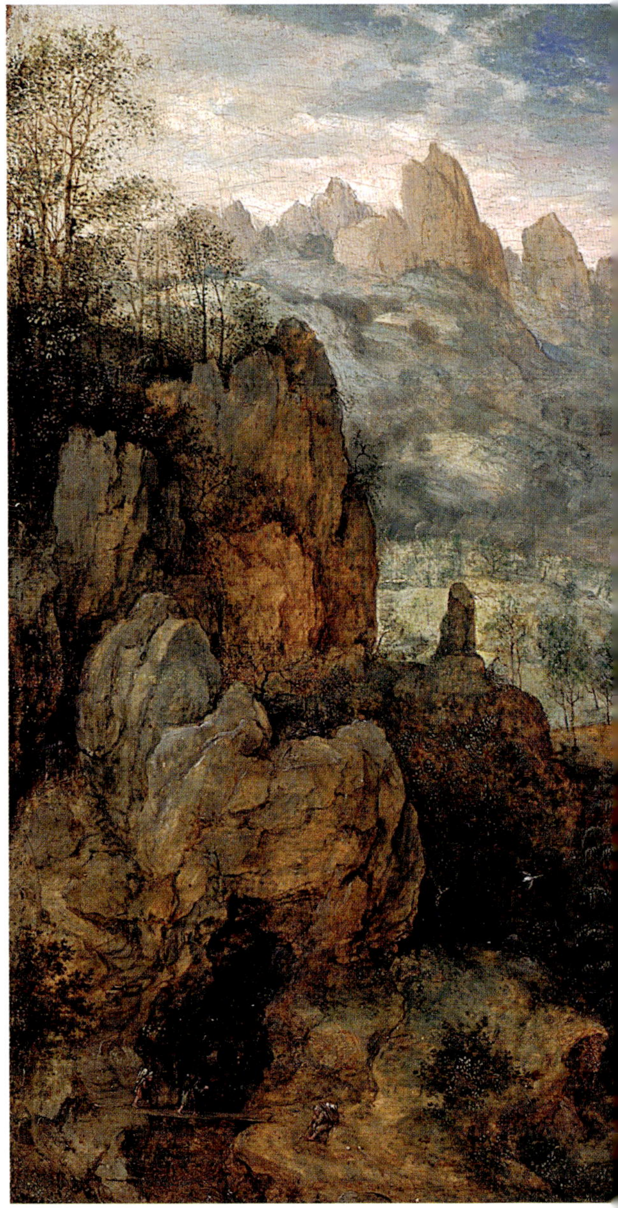

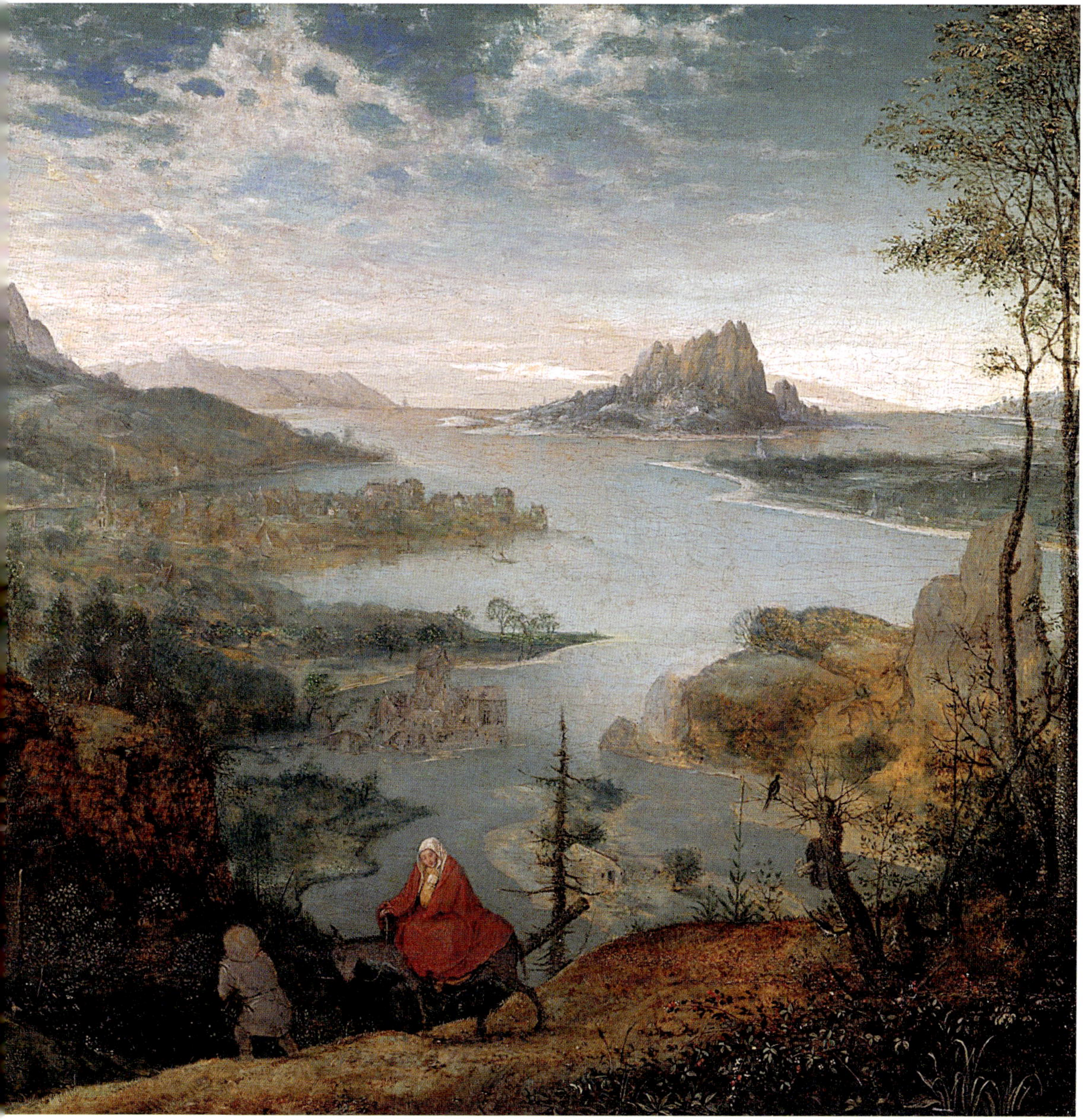

Landscape with the Flight into Egypt, 1563, Courtauld Gallery, London

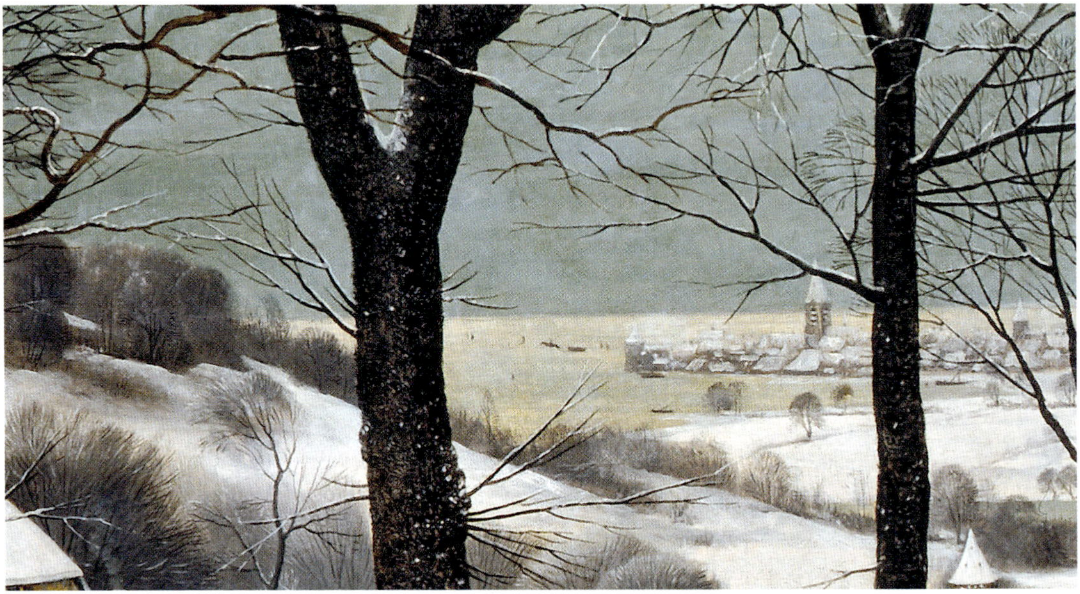

The Hunters in the Snow (detail), 1565, Kunsthistorisches Museum, Vienna

paintings as well. One of his compositional elements was colour which plays an important role in the world landscapes. The foreground is generally brownish, since the viewer is looking at the ground, while the middle distance is rendered in shades of green, with the background tending towards blue, according to general perception. Patinir had so perfectly mastered all this that Dürer praised him in his diary as a good "landscape painter", a designation he invented and one first applied to Patinir. And Dürer, as we know, knew what he was talking about.

Landscape itself was a popular picture subject in the Netherlands. It didn't matter whether it was real as long as it appeared to be so. The pictorial composition is such as later used by the German photographer Andreas Gursky (born 1955). Gursky describes his compositions as "unreal but realistic", and that is precisely what can be said of the landscapes of Pieter Bruegel. They give an impression of the size and grandeur of the world as well as the insignificance of mankind within it. In the Cycle of the Months he brought this to true mastery (pages 81, 83, 85). Bruegel goes far beyond the usual representations of months and seasons, which picture the annual cycle based on people's activities. He took a different approach, possibly as requested by his patron. For Jongelinck commissioned the cycle for the dining room in his country house, in which the paintings would hang nearly in a circle analogous to the cycle of the year with its constant changes and repetitions. There were to be six pictures in all, each one devoted to two consecutive months. The April and May picture has been lost. In Bruegel's works there is much to discover and they have much to relate—an important task of pictures, for elevated circles cultivated the "convivium", a dinner party graced by spirited conversation about literature, philosophy and art, a tradition previously recommended

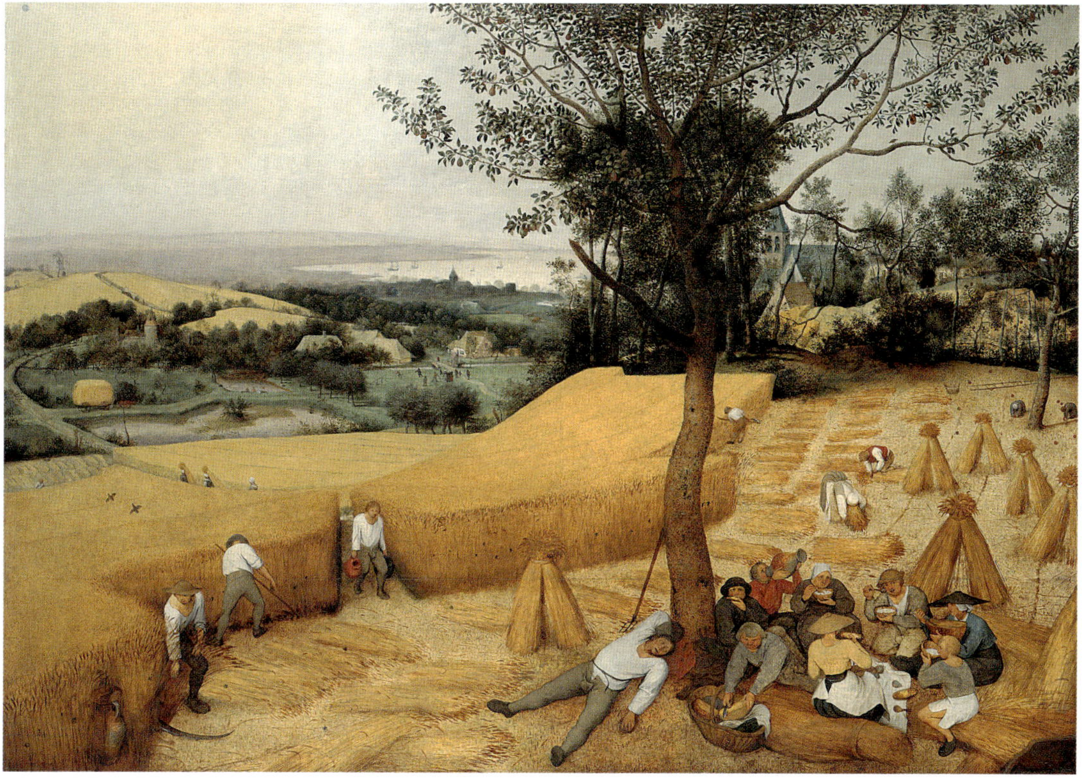

The Harvesters, 1565, The Metropolitan Museum of Art, New York

by Erasmus. And Bruegel's pictures provided any such gathering with ample subjects for conversation, for in them something new and in need of interpretation can always be discovered. But first and foremost the concept of these paintings is innovative, as instead of characterising the stages in the annual cycle by way of human activity, Bruegel does so primarily in terms of atmosphere by way of the colouring with which he infuses his "months". With its cool blue-green, metallic tones winter seems even visually frigid. But how cold it actually is can be seen from the ice-covered sea in the background (page 28). *The Harvesters* (above) is completely different; with its summery pale sky and yellow-gold wheat it exudes a pleasant warmth—one further enhanced by details such as the jug of beer hidden in the field, having been placed in the shade to keep it cool. The rainy brownish blue of late autumn ensures yet another different feeling to *The Return of the Herd* (pages 30/31). The motif of a herd of cows on a mountainside, unusual for flat Flanders, possibly harks back to Bruegel's journey across the Alps, where he surely would have been able to watch herds being driven up to or down the mountain pastures. By no means unusual, however, were the instruments of torture, the gallows and the wheel (page 32). Jongelinck's painting collection was appropriated

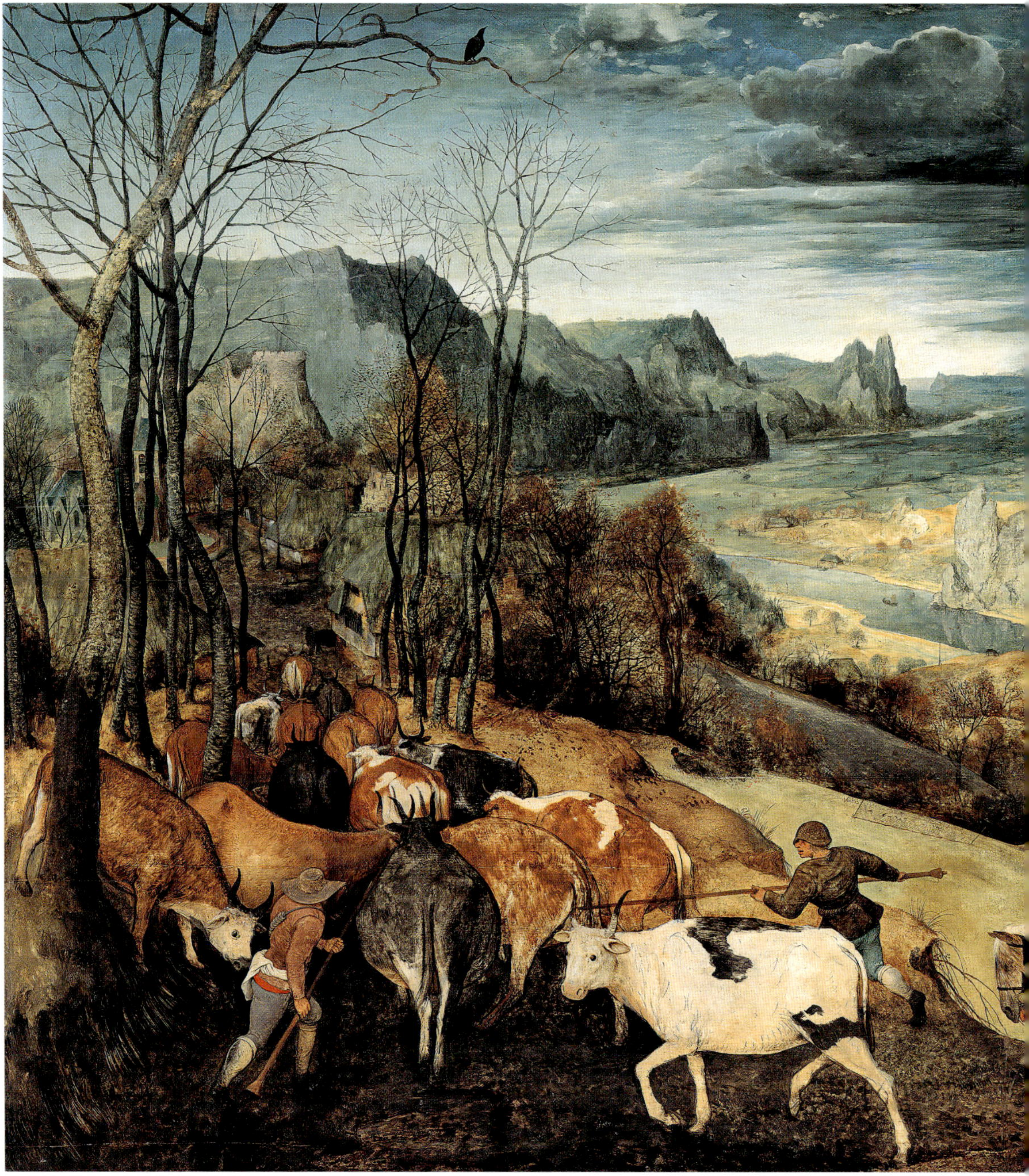

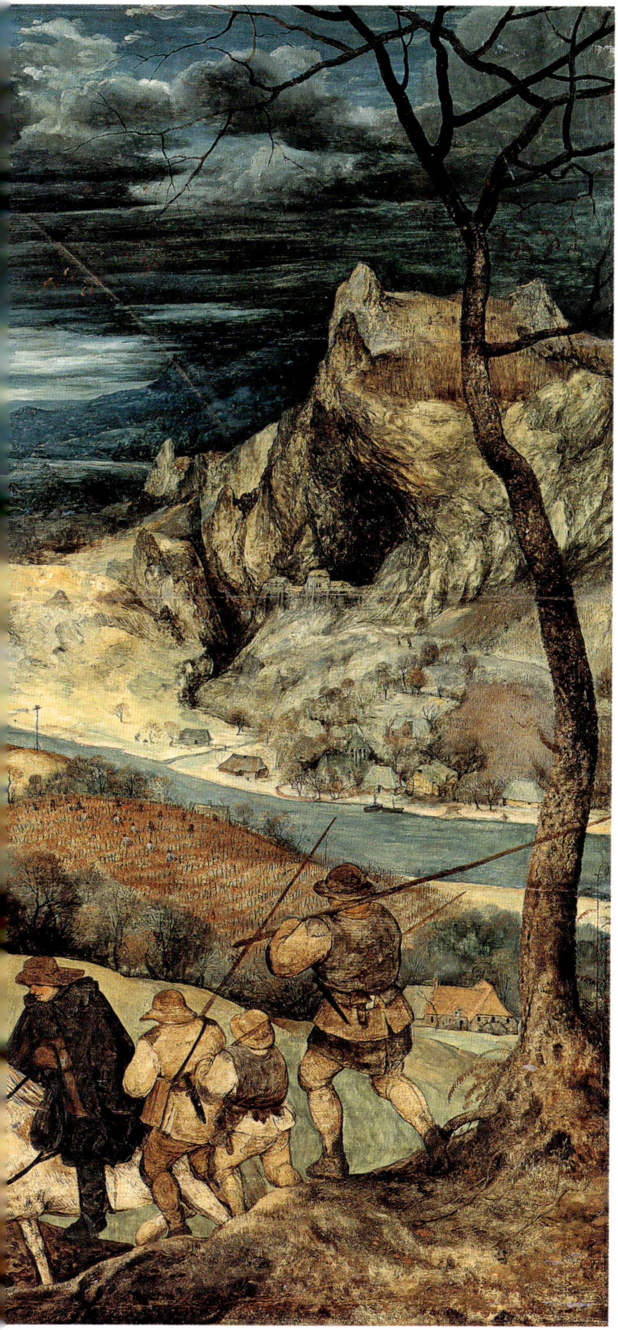

The Return of the Herd, 1565, Kunsthistorisches Museum, Vienna

by the city of Antwerp after its owner defaulted on his taxes. In 1594 they were presented to Archduke Ernst, brother of Emperor Rudolf II and governor of the Netherlands, which is how they found their way to Vienna, where three of them can still be seen today.

Municipal worthies were apparently often art collectors, as is shown by the example of Jan Noirot. He was Antwerp's mint master and a passionate collector with roughly fifty paintings, including five by Bruegel. In 1572 he went bankrupt, and abandoned his wife and children. His art collection was left behind and auctioned off in September of that year. Since lists were prepared on such occasions, we know that Noirot owned a winter landscape, two village fairs, and two peasant weddings by Bruegel (page 99).

These peasant scenes, for which the painter came to be misleadingly dubbed "Peasant Bruegel", were probably the pictures van Mander mentions in his biography of the artist: " . . . Bruegel often went out among the peasants dressed in country clothes when there was a fair or a wedding . . . he delighted in this, observing the peasants eating, drinking, dancing, leaping and courting in their own comical way, which he then wittily and amusingly mimicked in pigments . . . He understood how to faithfully capture peasant men and women . . . and the cloddish peasant nature in dancing, walking, standing and other movements". This may have seemed droll at the time, but now, at least, all the details that he included in these pictures seem anything but droll. It depends on how one looks at them.

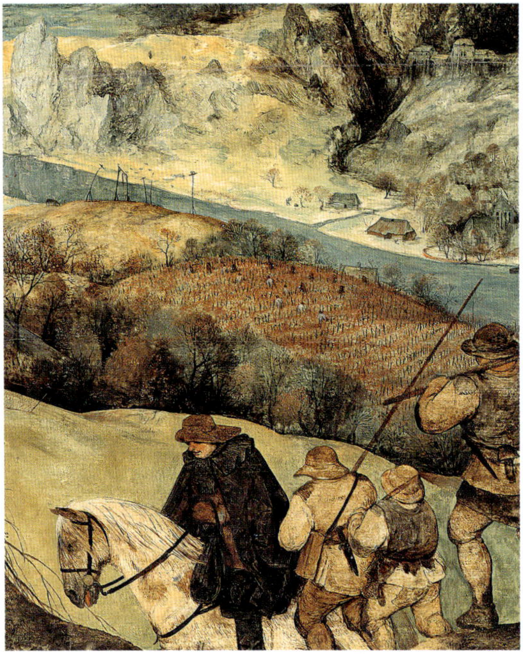

The Return of the Herd (detail)

Looking and perceiving are always of great importance in Bruegel's work in any case. For him non-seeing stands for a lack of understanding, which he portrays either by "hiding" important picture themes in the crowd or by means of pulled down hats or helmets, as in *The Conversion of Paul* (page 97), or even with thick glasses, as in *The Adoration of the Kings* (page 75) and the drawing *Painter and Connoisseur* (page 34). This drawing was long thought to include a self-portrait, which cannot be the case given his age at the time, for Bruegel would have been only in his late thirties. Moreover, he certainly would never, except possibly for underpaintings, have worked with such a brush. Instead, it appears that here he was commenting on the relationship between the painter and his undiscriminating but deep-pocketed client in general. Possibly even taking a jab at Catholic clients who were incapable of seeing and understanding his openly veiled allusions and criticisms even when they were standing right in front of them. In this context it could also be an homage to Hieronymus Bosch, who pictured such a figure in a somewhat different context in his painting *The Conjurer* from around 1502 (Musée Municipal, Saint-Germain-en-Laye).

Bruegel died in 1569. His last paintings *The Magpie on the Gallows* (page 107) and *The Peasant and the Nest Robber* (page 35) are very puzzling. There are no convincing interpretations of them to this day, only approaches. But this could have been Bruegel's intention, for the times were too dangerous for open criticism. According to van Mander's biography, it was not without reason that Bruegel directed his wife, who inherited the "Magpie painting", to burn certain pictures: "Many of his strange and elaborate allegories had been engraved, but he had made clean drawings of many more and provided them with inscriptions. Since they were too insulting and acrimonious, however, when he was on his deathbed, he had them burned by this wife, either because he regretted making them or because he feared that because of them, she could be faced with unpleasantness or called to account". Which ones these were cannot be known, of course, but that he was still capable of biting criticism late in life can be seen from the print *The Battle of the Moneybags and Strongboxes* (page 109), published posthumously.

Bruegel's subsequent fame was and is enormous. Considered by many to be the best painter in the Netherlands even during his lifetime, he came to be

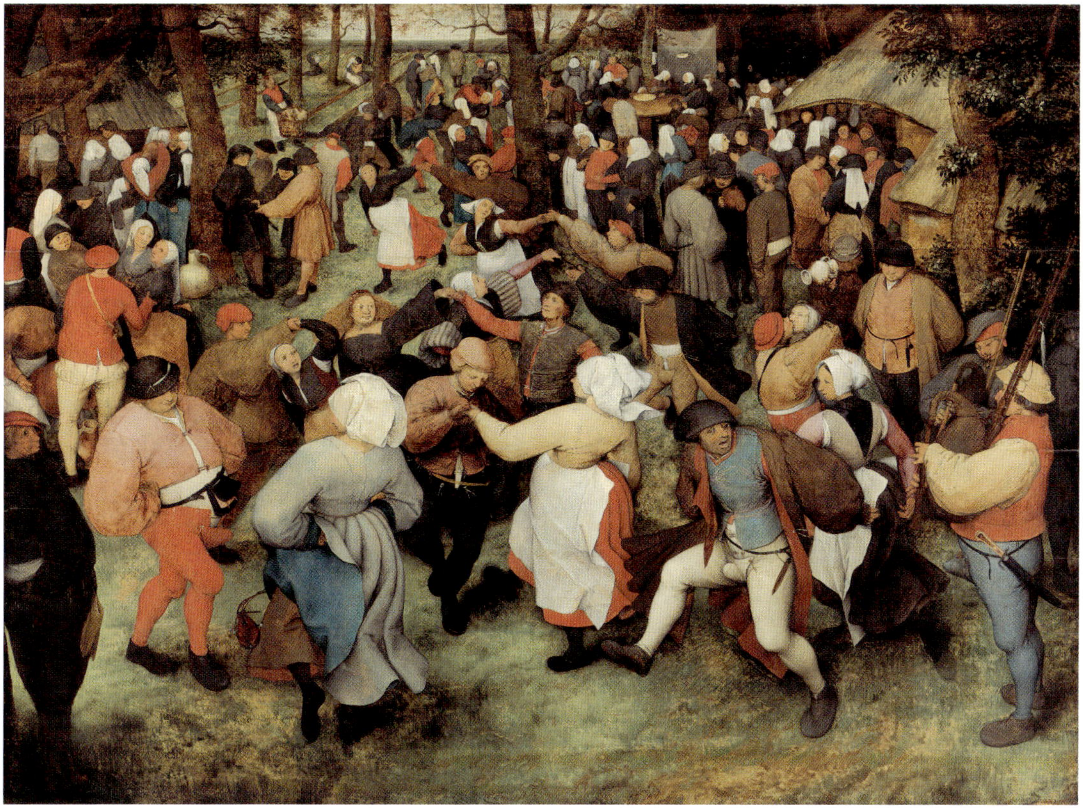

The Wedding Dance, c. 1566, Detroit Institute of Arts

even more highly celebrated after his death, as we see from the immediate increase in his prices. For example, in 1572 Granvelle's secretary Morillon purchased twenty-five paintings in Brussels for his collection but nothing more by Bruegel, for he had become too expensive even for a cardinal.

To meet the demand for Bruegel's works his sons produced copies. Jan Bruegel the Elder, his younger son, painted only a few; he specialised quite successfully in landscapes and floral still lifes, working with Peter Paul Rubens and others. Pieter the Younger, however, devoted his entire artistic career to his father's work. Both sons were too young to have been taught to paint by their father, so this was left to their grandmother. She had apparently preserved most of her son-in-law's preliminary drawings, cartoons and sketches, for only this would explain how Pieter the Younger managed to copy his father's works so precisely. At times this has also been of help in the interpretation of a work; one thinks, for example of *The Massacre of the Innocents* (pages 36/37 and page 87). Pieter the Younger ran a large workshop with nine assistants. In it as many as a hundred copies of specific paintings were produced. Absent in all of them, to be sure, is the ease of his

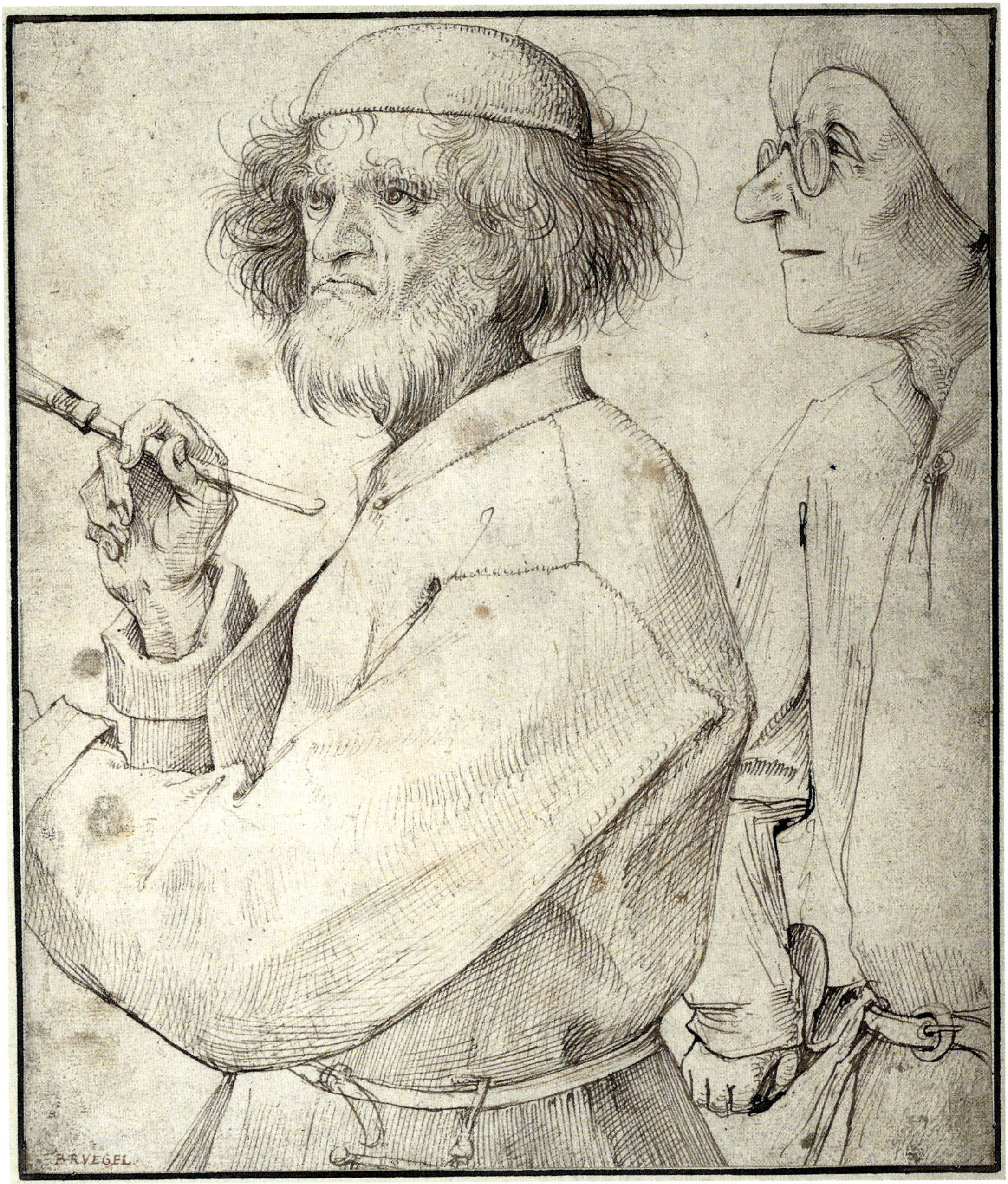

Painter and Connoisseur, c. 1565, Albertina, Vienna

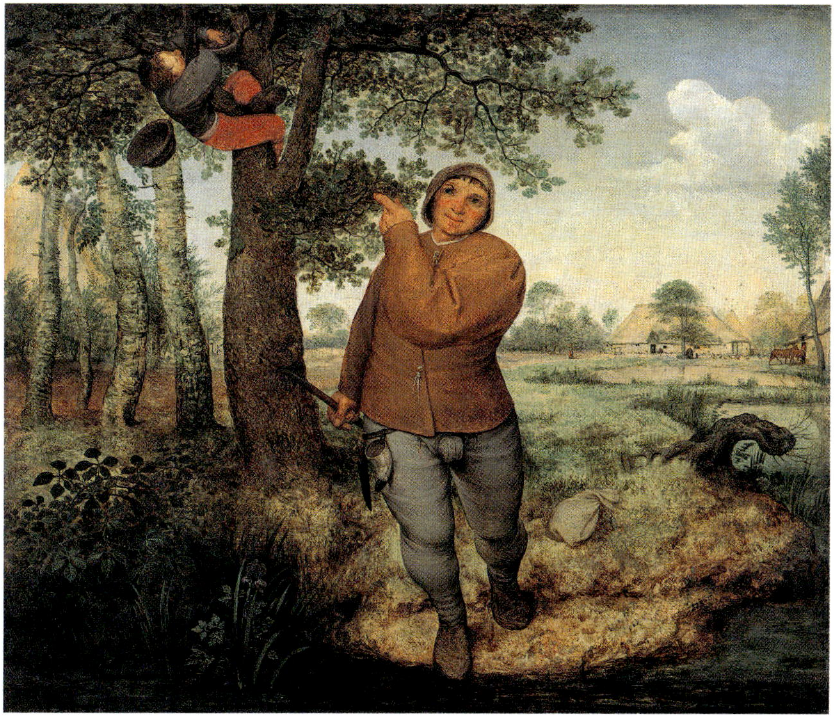

The Peasant and the Nest Robber, 1568, Kunsthistorisches Museum, Vienna

father's brush strokes, which he maintained despite his precision in even the smallest details.

Little is known about Pieter Bruegel the Elder as a man, nor about his actual intentions in his art. But from his drawings and paintings his view of the world can be sensed. That world had been expanded by a new continent, one whose novelties he could admire in his hometown. He was one of the most popular artists in his own country and one of the best known in the whole of Europe. He saw the beginning of capitalism and recognised its dangers; he experienced the misuses of power and religion and pictured them in his work. He stood as an observer on the fringes and as a citizen in the thick of a complicated and dangerous world where a false religion (whichever it was) could mean being sent to the gallows. He depicted this world in all its complexity and contradictions, with all its burdens and desires, in a manner that gives us much to think about to this day.

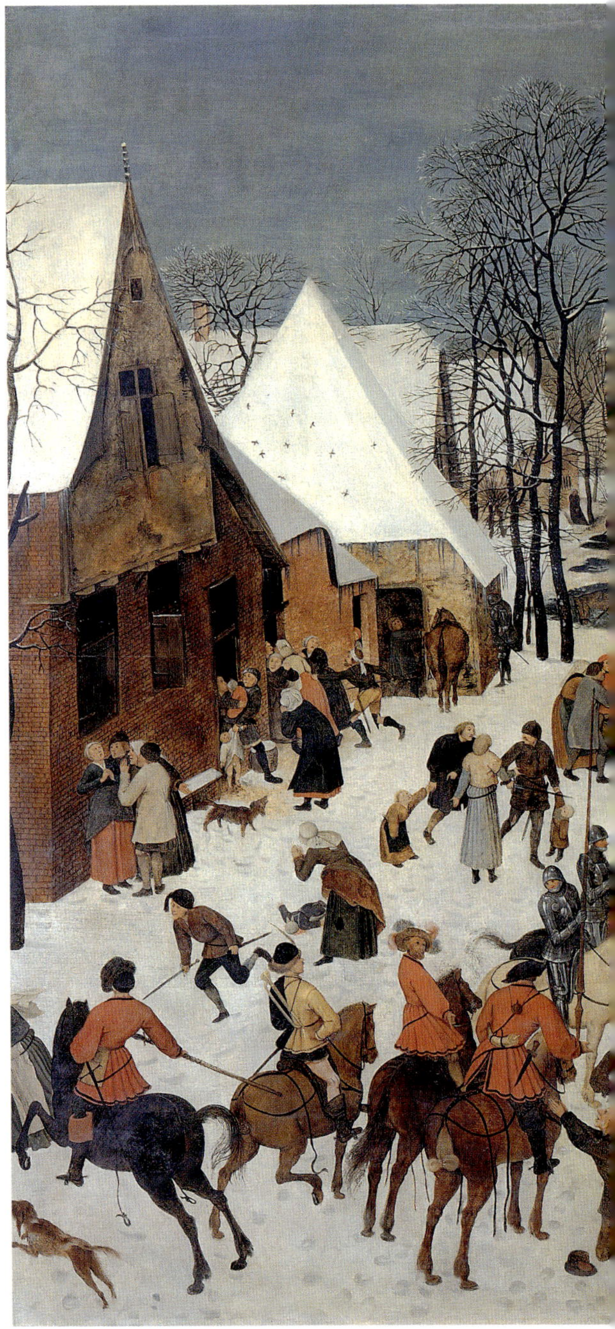

The Massacre of the Innocents, copy by Pieter Bruegel the Younger, 4th quarter of the 16th century, Kunsthistorisches Museum, Vienna

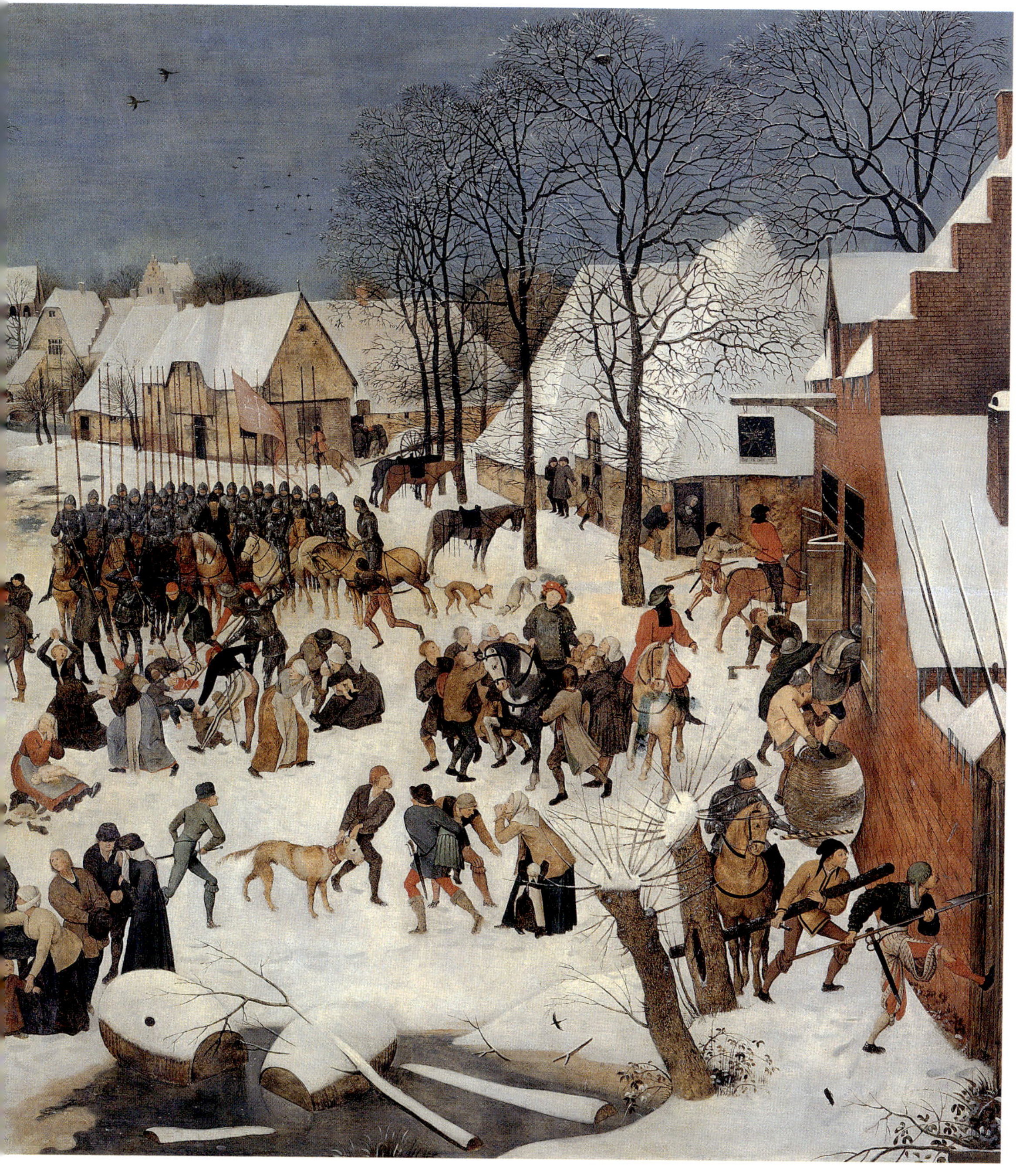

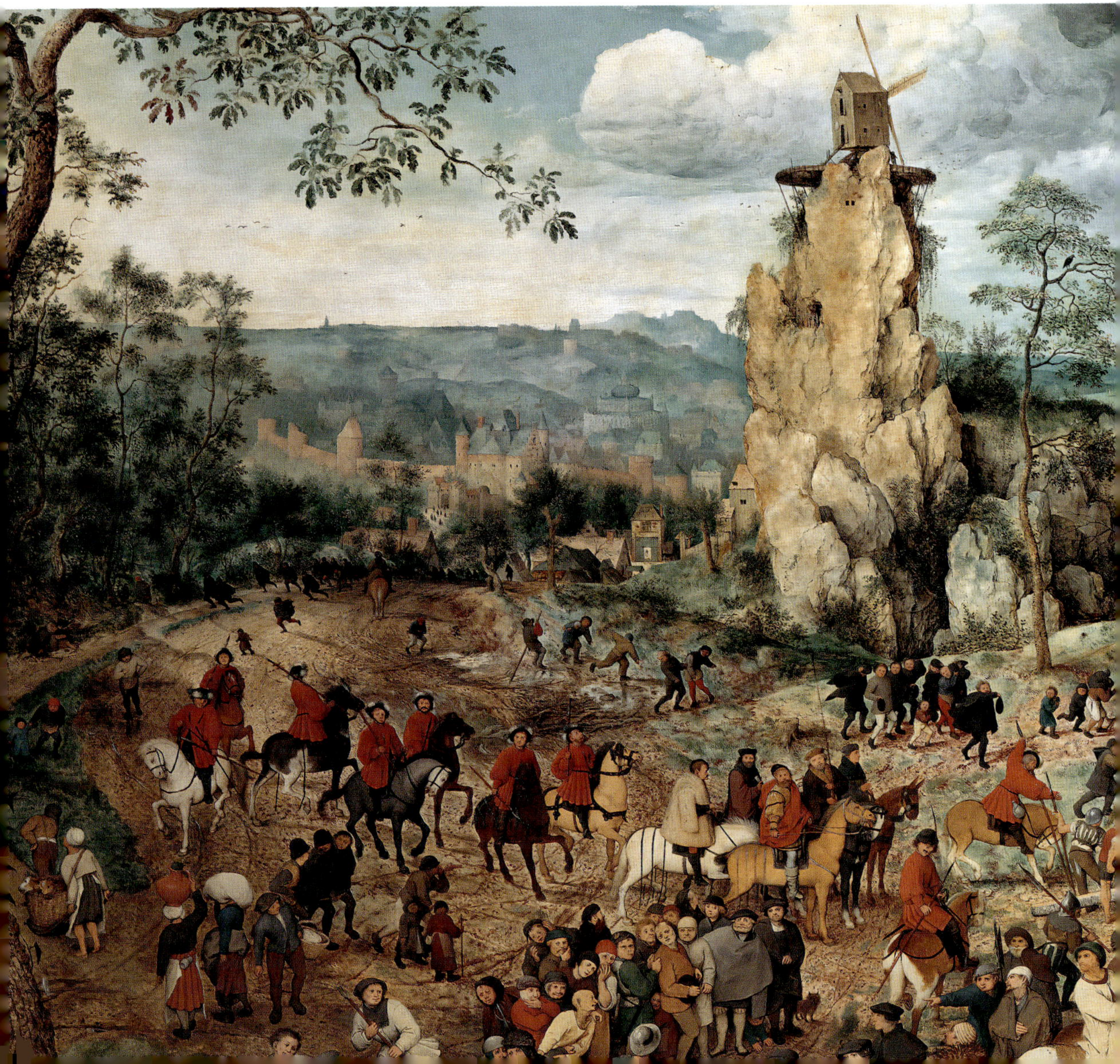

WORKS

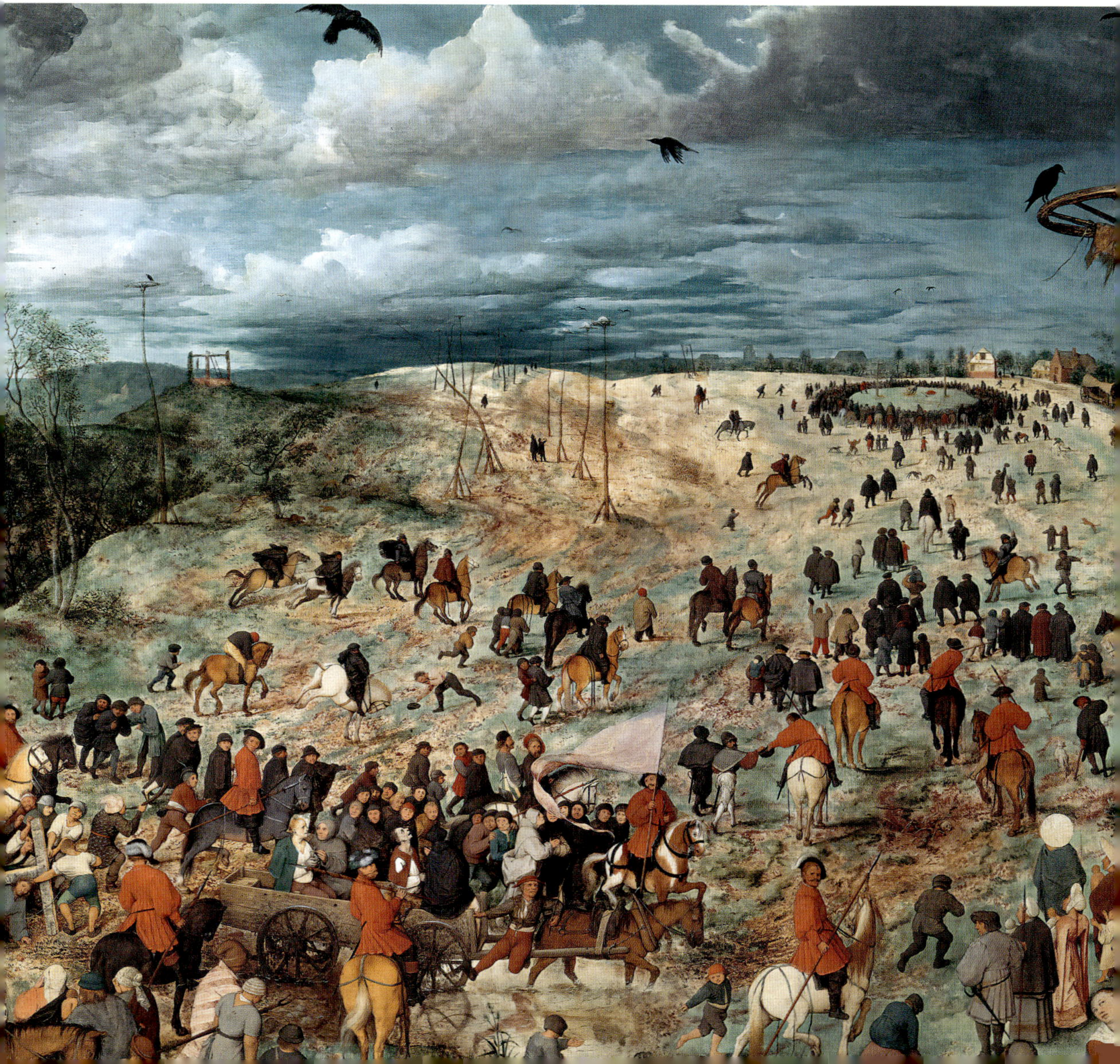

The Temptation of Saint Antony, c. 1556

Pen and brown ink on paper
21.6 × 32.6 cm
Ashmolean Museum, Oxford

The Temptation of Saint Anthony has always been a subject tempting artists to indulge their fantasies. From Hieronymus Bosch to Herri met de Bles to Salvador Dalí (1904–1989), many have tried their hand at it. Anthony (presumedly 251–356), the son of well-to-do farmers, followed the call of Christ after the death of his parents: "If thou wilt be perfect, go sell what thou hast, and give to the poor, and thou shalt have treasure in heaven: and come follow me" (Matthew 19:21). So he gave away his wealth and withdrew as a hermit into the desert, where he was constantly plagued by visions sent by the devil. The devil appeared to him as a giant or showed him seductive women and monstrous creatures. The devil also wanted to entice him with gold, silver and other riches, which was naturally an invitation to artists to exercise their imaginations. In Bruegel's drawing one still sees the great influence the beloved and popular Hieronymus Bosch had on the art of his successor. The sheet is filled with the cast of monsters from Bosch's world, like the huge head as the gate to hell, the outsize fish and hybrid figures composed of various human and other components. On the engraving produced after the drawing and sold by Hieronymus Cock, the name Bruegel does not appear. Possibly the publisher hoped to exploit the continuing popularity of Bosch and sell larger editions than he would have been able to with a still unknown artist like Bruegel. But Bruegel had definitely set his own accents. In the upper right, for example, one sees a crossbowman taking aim at the hermit and a female lutenist in the hollow of the tree lures him with her body and her music. Also in the tree hollow lies a pig, an Anthony attribute, for he is also the patron saint of swineherds. According to legend, the pig had the job of reminding him when it was time to pray. A more important difference from many other versions is Bruegel's landscape. It is clearly no desert, but a perfectly idyllic river landscape with villages along its banks. The reason for this could have been a local crisis at the time, for in the year the drawing was made the plague broke out in Beveren, on the bank of the Schelde opposite Antwerp. Perhaps this immediate menace prompted Bruegel to combine it with that of the devil in the legend of the saint.

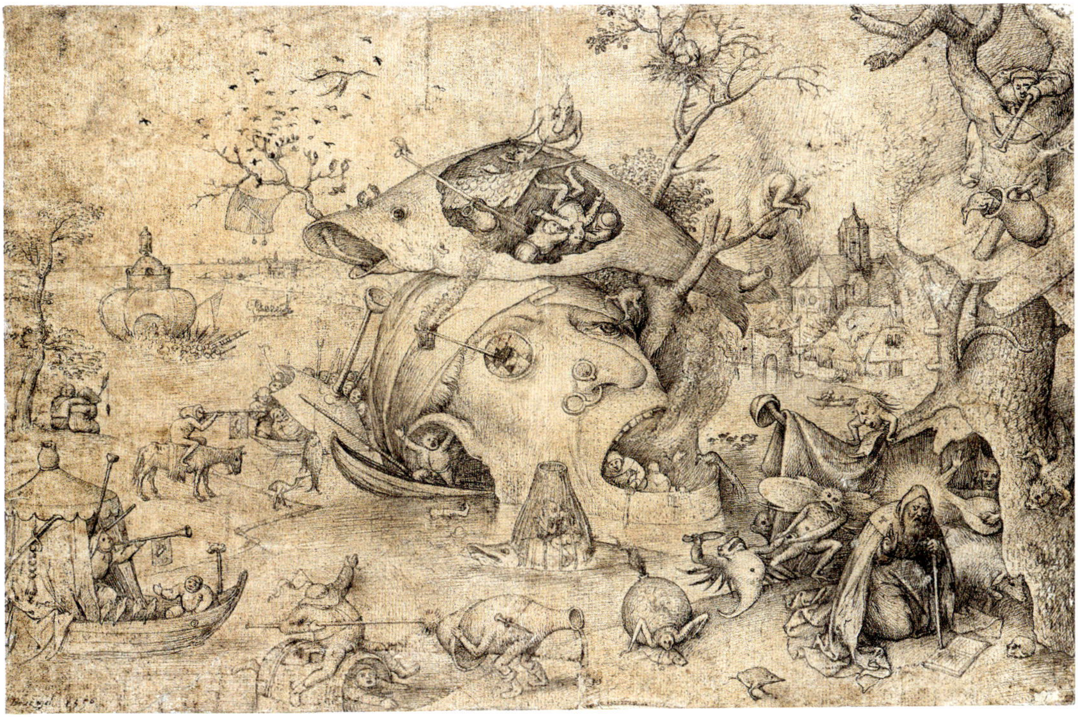

Big Fish Eat Little Fish, 1557

Engraving by Pieter van der Heyden
22.9 × 29.6 cm
The Metropolitan Museum of Art, New York

The viewer is presented with a bizarre scene on a seashore where two men are cutting open and "processing" a giant fish. They are being watched by a man and a child, probably father and son, seated in a boat belonging to a fisherman who is himself gutting a fish. Behind the huge fish stands a fisherman's hut with the resident fishermen hanging up their catch, several large fish, to dry. On a small island in the background people have gathered around another gigantic fish. On the horizon one can see a bustling coastal city. Out of the fish being cut up in the foreground pour heaps of smaller fish and from their mouths slither still smaller ones. The man with the absurdly large knife is equipped like a knight with helmet, vambraces and greaves. Engraved on the knife blade is a sphaira, a Christian world symbol that would stand upside-down if the man were to hold the knife the other way—symbol of a world that is also upside-down, driven by greed and avarice. This refers directly to the picture's title: *Big Fish Eat Little Fish*, eat and be eaten—a truism known long before Bruegel and one that has lost none of its validity to this day. And it is precisely this sobering fact that the father appears to want to point out to his son. With the "ecce" ("look") he calls the boy's attention to this pessimistic basic principle. The viewer unconsciously appends to the "ecce" the word "homo", which in this case refers not to Christ but to men in general, who profitably participate in this food chain of which they stand at the top. The second word is lacking in Bruegel's drawing. Whether the idea of including the "ecce" came from Bruegel, the engraver Pieter van der Heyden or the publisher Hieronymus Cock, is unclear. As publisher, Cock had the last word in any case. He was the author of the Latin titles important for international sales, also the sentence in Flemish placed in the mouth of the father: "Look, son, I have known for a long time that the big fish eat the little ones". And Cock was also responsible for the signature, which does not read "Bruegel", for example, but "Hieronymus Bos. Inventor"—unlike the preliminary drawing. The most probable reason for this was the chance for increased sales, for Bosch's works were still greatly sought after. Here too the big fish (Bosch) devours the—still—smaller fish (Bruegel).

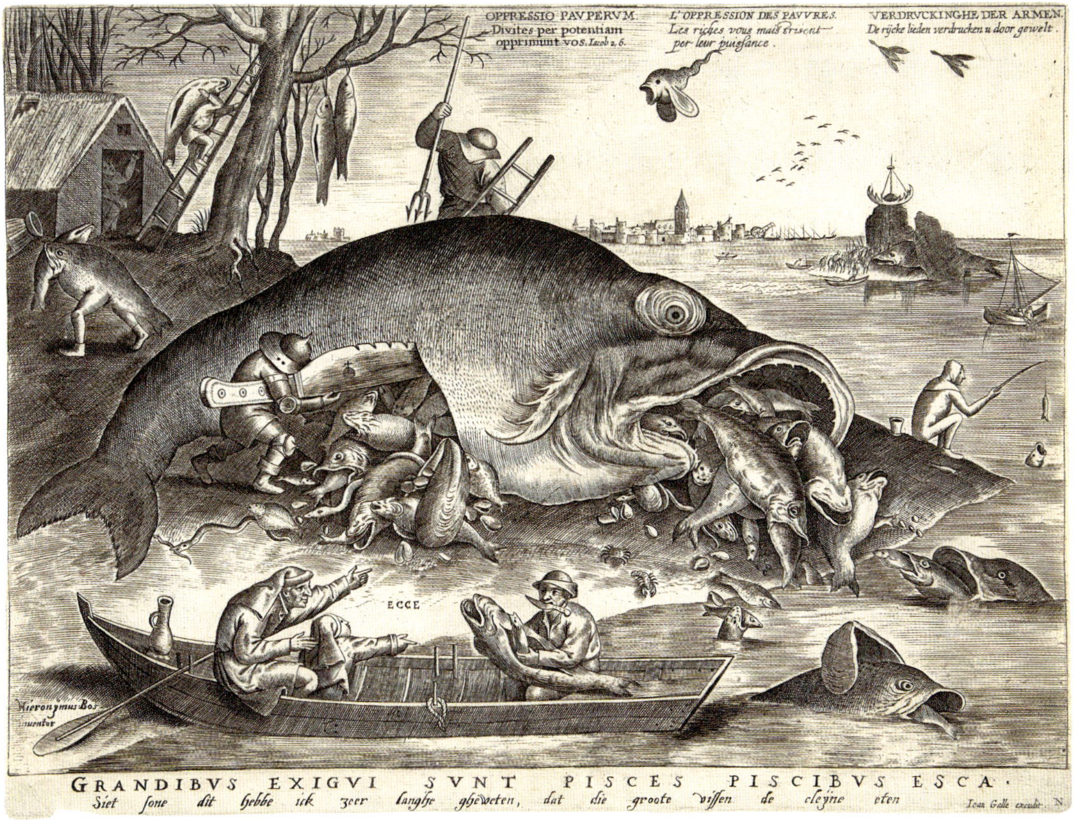

OPPRESSIO PAVPERVM.
Divites per potentiam opprimunt vos. Iacob 2, 6.
L'OPPRESSION DES PAVVRES.
Les riches vous mais brisent per leur puissance.
VERDRVCKINGHE DER ARMEN.
De rijcke lieden verdrucken u door gewelt.
ECCE
Hieronymus Bos inventor
GRANDIBVS EXIGVI SVNT PISCES PISCIBVS ESCA.
Siet sone dit hebbe ick zeer langhe ghewetën, dat die groote vissen de cleyne eten
Ioan Galle excudit. N

Superbia (Pride), 1558

Engraving by Pieter van der Heyden
22.5 × 29.5 cm
The Metropolitan Museum of Art, New York

With his print of Superbia, the sin of pride, Bruegel appears to have anticipated the selfie craze of our own time. The sin of pride is man's presumptuous overestimation of himself, even with regard to his external appearance. Isidor of Seville (c. 560–636), one of the most widely read Christian writers of the Middle Ages, wrote that the proud distinguish themselves by wishing to seem more than they are. One expression of pride is a vain and hollow search for fame. For his personification of pride Bruegel pictures an elegantly dressed, conceited woman holding up her attribute, a mirror. She is accompanied by a peacock—an additional attribute—that has fanned out its imposing tail feathers. Filling the picture are multiple bizarre figures, all of which exhibit self-love and vanity. Most important to these creatures is the mirror in which they love to admire and see a version of themselves that they—but only they—find beautiful. The foreground toad-like figure with a fish's tail has adorned himself with a peacock feather and has pierced his lips for a ring. The woman behind him holding his mirror appears to be a nun, but she cannot completely hide beneath her clothing the fact that she is actually a monster. Another figure next to the toad-like creature has assumed a highly contorted pose that allows him to see himself and his behind in a mirror—and find it gorgeous. If one mentally substitutes mobile phones for the mirrors in this picture one very quickly lands in the present day. Next to the peacock the shop of a barber can be seen who has the task of making his customers look their best. It appears that he also sells mirrors on the side. A cleric on a horse behind Superbia seems to be worrying about his vanity incognito. In Superbia's retinue there are also tailors and a weird shepherd with the face of an animal who is presenting a naked young woman to a lady. The shepherd can be seen as a symbol of the Church, though the sword beneath his cloak hardly sheds a favourable light on that institution. In the background Bruegel depicts fantastic structures, more than in any other picture, whose roofs are reminiscent of such clerical objects as censers, cardinals' hats and tiaras. The print's inscription reads: "Pride is hated by God more than anything and at the same time God is scorned by the proud". The second half of that statement seems only logical, for one assumes that the proud see only themselves as the supreme being.

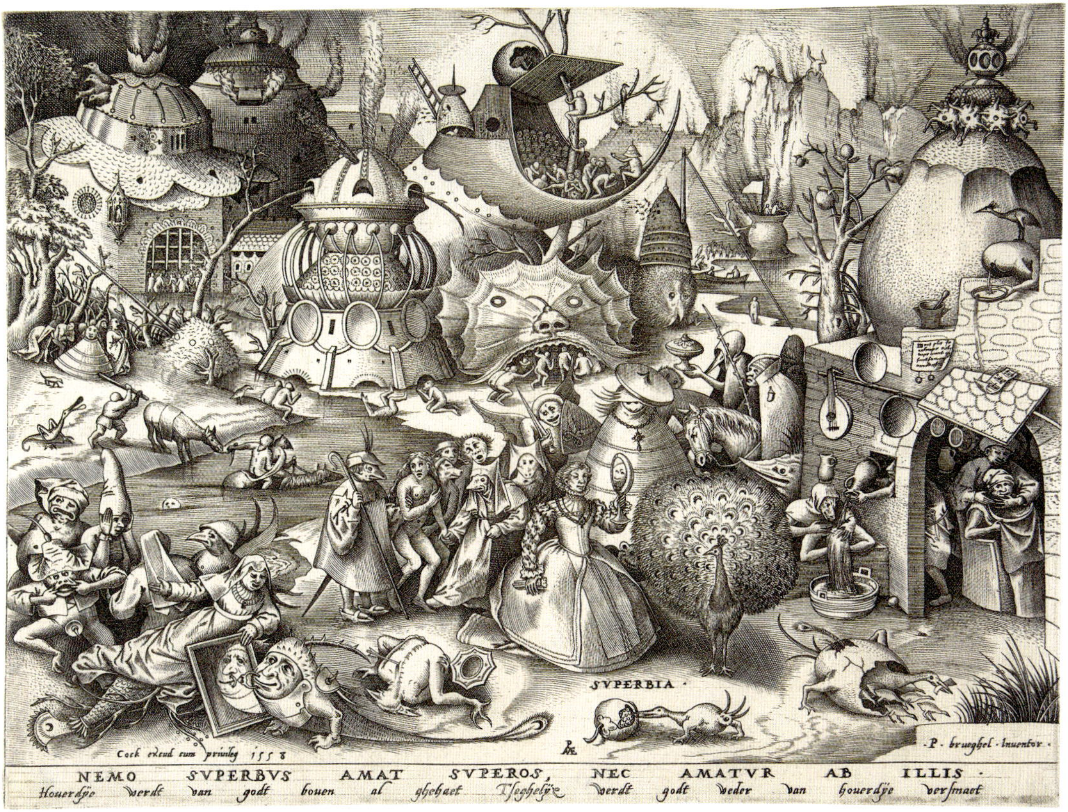
SVPERBIA ·
Cock excud cum priuileg 1558
· P · brueghel · Inuentor ·
NEMO SVPERBVS AMAT SVPEROS, NEC AMATVR AB ILLIS ·
Houerdye werdt van godt bouen al ghehaet Tseghelye werdt godt weder van houerdye versmaet

Justitia, 1559/60

Engraving by Philipp Galle
26 × 33.5 cm
The Metropolitan Museum of Art, New York

This illustration of the virtue of justice is one of the most powerful and most brutal prints Bruegel ever produced. In its vividness it is exceeded only by his painting *The Triumph of Death* (page 61). One could almost regard the scene as a primer for torturers and executioners. Yet Justitia stands on a pedestal with her familiar attributes of a scale, a sword and the blindfold that ensures that she reaches her judgments without regard to the status of the accused. She is simply ignored, however. And because of the blindfold she also fails to see anything else—even what horrors are being committed in her name. Right at her feet—and one has to imagine that she can hear his agonised cries—a delinquent is being sadistically tortured: with great effort the torturer is stretching him on a rack while litres of water are being funnelled into his mouth—an early form of waterboarding. In addition, another henchman is nonchalantly dripping hot wax onto his bare legs. But this is only the beginning: on the podium behind, a man is about to be beheaded and farther back another one is being flogged to the delight of a crowd while a third hangs upside down with his hands and feet tied together. In the hall one person's hand is being chopped off while the next victim stands in line. And in the right foreground sits some bureaucrat making sure that everything is proceeding smoothly and accurate records are being kept. As if this were not enough, what is taking place in the background is even more extreme. Corpses hang from the gallows and other condemned souls are dying on wheels, while on the right an enthusiastic crowd is watching a person being burned alive—the usual punishment for "heretics". Across from this on the left one can make out a crucifixion group with Mary and John—Bruegel's commentary on the "legality" of the proceedings. In the left foreground scholars are debating, among them probably John Calvin, who had the humanist and religious freethinker Michel Servetus burned at the stake in 1553: religious intolerance was not limited to Catholics. The accompanying text makes the scene seem even more absurd: "The aim of the law is to either improve the person it punishes or with his punishment make other people better, or so that after the evil doers are eliminated others can live in greater safety". None of this is realised here. What is happening here is not justice but only punitive violence. No acquittals, no clemency and no grace. It is a glimpse into the cruelty of Bruegel's time—conditions as they existed in unjust regimes back then as they still do today.

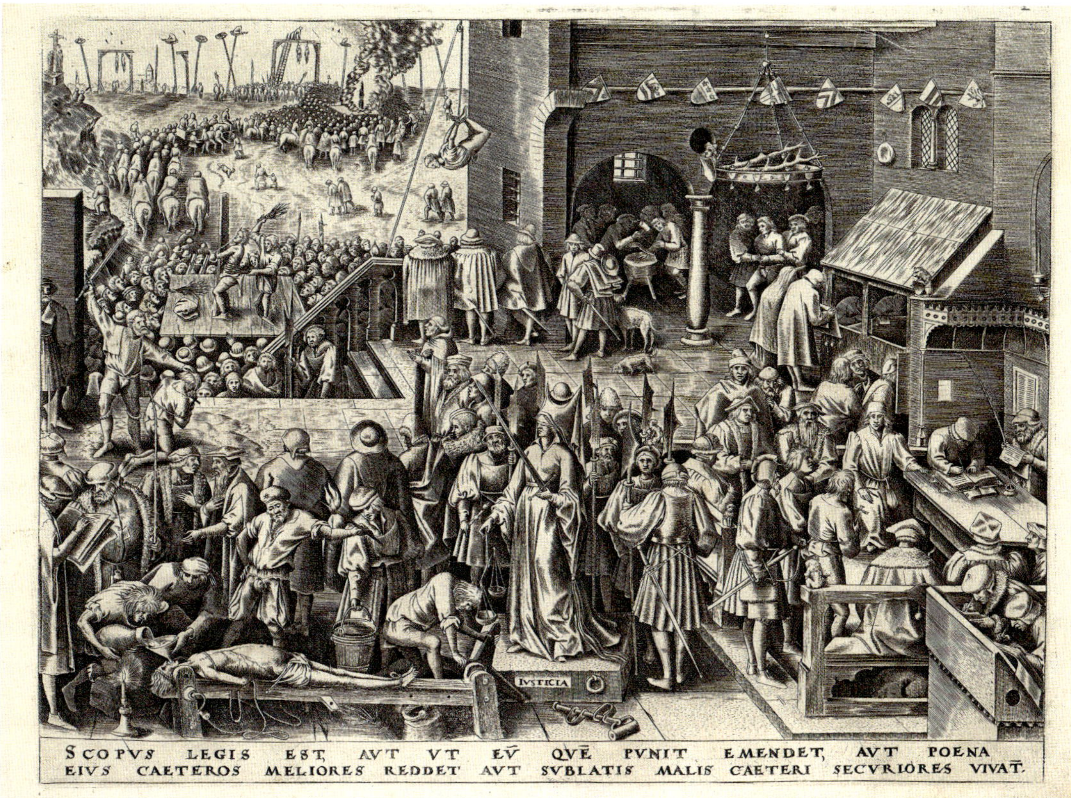
IVSTICIA
SCOPVS LEGIS EST, AVT VT EV̄ QVĒ PVNIT EMENDET, AVT POENA
EIVS CAETEROS MELIORES REDDET AVT SVBLATIS MALIS CAETERI SECVRIORES VIVAT.

Elck, c. 1558

Engraving by Pieter van der Heyden
24.7 × 29.5 cm
The Metropolitan Museum of Art, New York

This print narrates the story of "Elck", or Everyman: at the end of his life the rich man realises that all his accumulated possessions cannot save him from death. It is a story dating back to medieval mystery plays and one that enjoys great popularity to this day. The best-known version is Hugo von Hofmannsthal's *Jedermann*, performed annually in Salzburg. In Bruegel's version Elck is characterised as a merchant by the quill behind his ear, his glasses and of course his bag of money. Surrounded by all manner of tools, merchandise, gaming boards, dice and other diversion techniques of which he has apparently lost an overview, he is searching for something and carrying a lantern—in broad daylight. What he is looking for is explained in the accompanying text: "There is no one who does not look everywhere for his advantage, no one who does not seek himself in all that he does, no one who does not see everywhere only his own benefit. This one here and that one there lug something home and all have a single love: the love of ownership". The picture shows that the search for material goods is misleading in the picture of the fool with a mirror who says: "No one knows himself". Bruegel emphasises the desperation of the man's search by showing him multiple times: he looks in sacks, baskets, in the military and the Church (both in the background) and argues with himself whenever he thinks he has found something—visualised in the "tug of war" on the left. That it is everywhere the same Elck, that all are Elck, is indicated by the word "Elck" appearing on the hems of their skirts. On that of the central Elck it also appears in Latin and French for the international public. The lamp as an aid in his search recalls the Greek philosopher Diogenes (c. 412–323 B.C.), of whom it is said that on the marketplace in the middle of the day he sought virtuous men—and found none. Bruegel underscores the reference in that he has his protagonist also search in a barrel, Diogenes's residence. And of course Elck fails to find in the exterior, material world what is only present in the interior one. Whether this is the true faith, in Bruegel's time a constant concern, or self-knowledge is left up to the viewer to decide. What neither occurs to Elck nor delays him in his search is the fact that he has tripped over a sphaira, a Christian world symbol, and not only upset it, or brought the world into disorder, but virtually destroyed it.

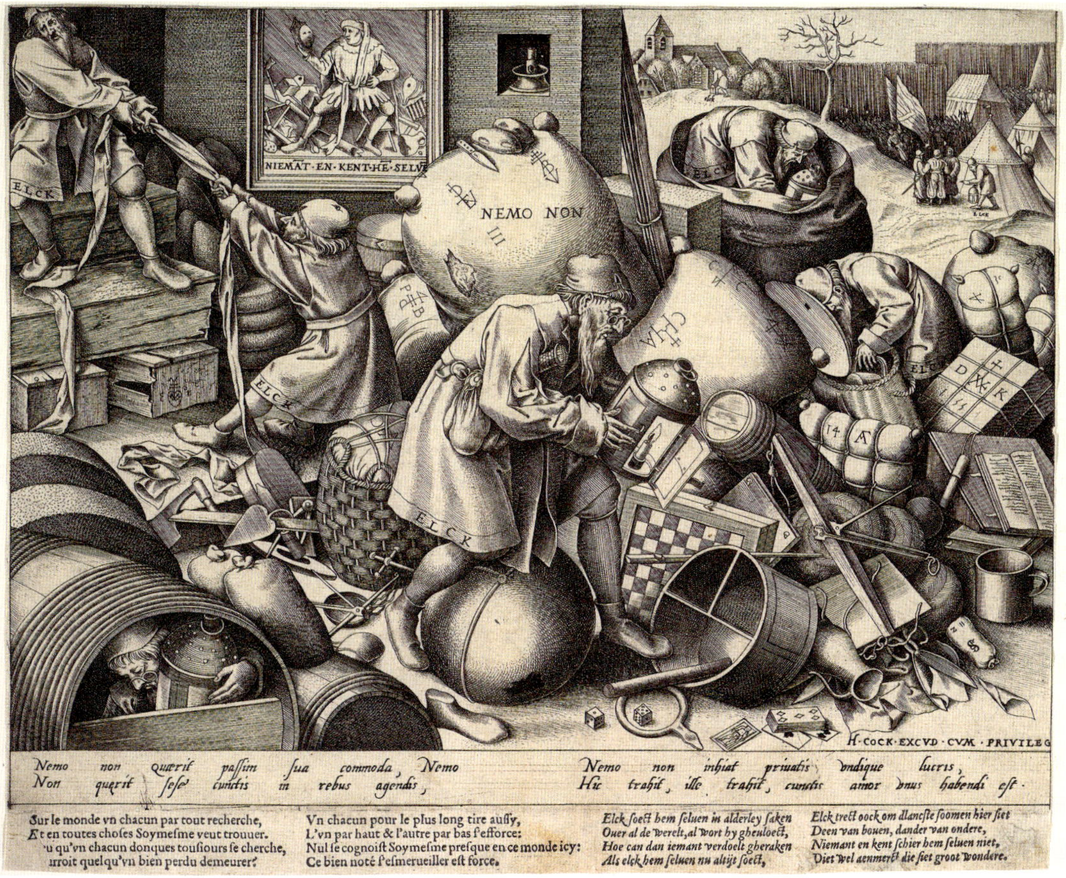
NIEMAT·EN·KENT·HE·SELVE
NEMO NON
ELCK
H·COCK·EXCVD·CVM·PRIVILEG
Nemo non quærit passim sua commoda, Nemo
Non quærit sese cunctis in rebus agendis,
Nemo non inhiat priuatis vndique lucris,
Hic trahit, ille trahit, cunctis amor vnus habendi est.
Sur le monde vn chacun par tout recherche,
Et en toutes choses Soymesme veut trouuer.
·u qu'vn chacun donques tousiours se cherche,
ırroit quelqu'vn bien perdu demeurer?
Vn chacun pour le plus long tire aussy,
L'vn par haut & l'autre par bas s'efforce:
Nul se cognoist Soymesme presque en ce monde icy:
Ce bien noté s'esmerueiller est force.
Elck soect hem seluen in alderley saken
Ouer al de werelt, al wort hy gheuloect,
Hoe can dan iemant verdoelt gheraken
Als elck hem seluen nu altijt soect,
Elck treckt oock om dlancste soomen hier siet
Deen van bouen, dander van ondere,
Niemant en kent schier hem seluen niet,
Diet wel aenmerct die siet groot wondere.

Netherlandish Proverbs, 1559

Oil on oak panel
117.2 × 263.8 cm
Staatliche Museen zu Berlin, Gemäldegalerie

In a seaside village the inhabitants are carrying out strange activities, the sense of which is not immediately apparent. A full 119 proverbs are illustrated, by means of which the viewer is introduced into an oddly topsy-turvy world. That appears to be the motto, also symbolised by the globe seen time and again in Bruegel's pictures, here hanging upside-down against the wall of the house. And this world is hardly improved by the fact that the fool hanging his bare behind out the window above is shitting on it. Bruegel has created an image of a wacky world. His view appears to have been shaped by a profound pessimism, for humankind is apparently not in a position to set the world straight. The viewer is first struck by the woman in a red dress draping a blue cloak around an old man. "Draping a blue cloak around a person" meant deceiving and hoodwinking him. But it also meant self-deception and, as the cause of misfortune and sin, was associated with such concepts as foolishness and a "topsy-turvy world" as Bruegel had already pictured it in *Elck* (page 49). Proverbs were greatly in vogue; Bruegel's painting was preceded by a popular engraving by Frans Hogenberg: *The Blue Cloak* (c. 1558), in which he illustrated some forty proverbs and provided them with labels. Bruegel's picture was so popular that his son Pieter produced at least sixteen copies of it. Erasmus of Rotterdam with his *In Praise of Folly* (1511) and Sebastian Brandt with his *Ship of Fools* (1494) had already dealt most successfully with the subject of foolishness. In his repeatedly reprinted book *Adagia* Erasmus had also collected a total of 4,251 proverbs and idioms from antiquity up to his own time. From common ones like "wanting to put your head through the wall" to examples unknown today like "the sow pulls the bung out" ("Negligence will be rewarded with disaster"), all manner of proverbs are pictured in Bruegel's painting. The difficulty was transferring figurative language into imagery, as one had to take a decision such as in the example "hanging a flaxen beard around God" (centre right) which means that deceit often takes place behind the mask of sanctimoniousness, as it is not said who is doing it. Bruegel decided on a monk, which definitely implies criticism of the clergy. Aside from all that is pictured in it, this painting is a masterpiece of composition, colouring and manipulation of the viewer's gaze. Despite the absurdities, everything appears to follow an inner logic, in which the illustration of the proverbs and the requisite architecture and surroundings give rise to each other. What will the people in this village do once the painter and viewer have gone? Will they go back to their everyday activities or remain forever trapped in this preposterous, hopelessly ludicrous world?

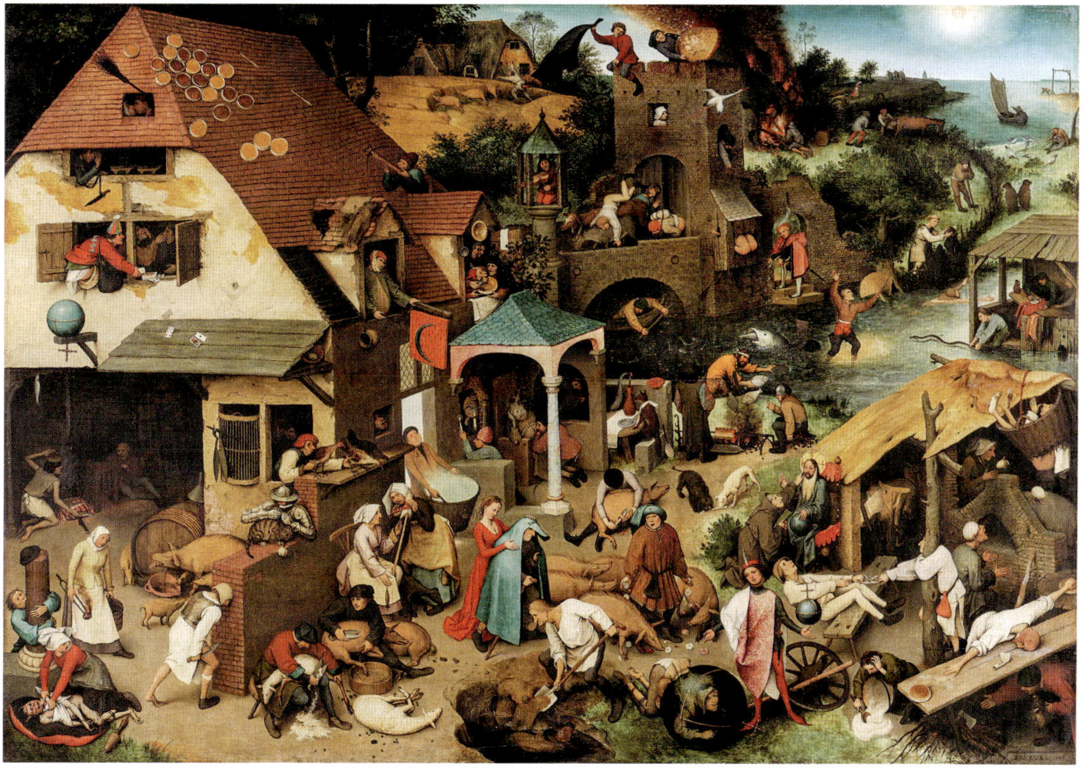

The Fight Between Carnival and Lent, 1559

Oil on oak panel
118 × 163.7 cm
Kunsthistorisches Museum, Vienna

Carnival revels have begun in a city; between the church and the tavern people are engaged in their traditional antics. In the foreground one sees the struggle between Carnival and the fasting during Lent that gives the picture its title. Plump Carnival is riding on a barrel pushed by a pair of clowns. His train is escorted by a pair of masked men playing music who are bringing candles and a set table to the "fight". His lance is a spit skewered with a suckling pig, a chicken and sausages. Across from him Lent, personified by an emaciated old woman in a grey dress, is being drawn along on a cart. Her "lance" is a baker's paddle holding two meagre fish. On the left next to the tavern, "At the Blue Barque", a well-known clowning and Carnival brotherhood in Antwerp, a play is being performed. Above, in front of it, another one is in progress—fun and inebriation for all. On the right, by contrast, clerical sobriety dominates with repentance, alms and Lenten fare like pretzels, breads and mussels. The personifications of Carnival and Lent can also be read as contrasts between the Catholic and Lutheran Churches. Between them children are playing and cripples are trying to call attention to themselves. A female pilgrim with a hat and a basket appears to want to help them. In her basket, however, one can see a monkey, generally seen as a symbol for deception. Bruegel is here depicting customs actually identifiable in folklore, but as so often gives his special view of the world, with all the joys and all sorrows—until death, which has been deleted by later overpaintings. In the infrared photograph one can see in the right foreground a white cloth that only half covered a later overpainted corpse. In front of the table next to the church entrance lay two dying children, who were also overpainted like the corpse in the tumbrel pulled by the woman next to it. Carnival is a utopia and an outlet, a reversal of the world both imaginary and actual. For a certain period anarchy rules, people can let off steam and criticism is tolerated. Bruegel lived in a time of repression and restraint, one in which such freedoms were increasingly limited. The mayhem is being watched by a puppet seated at the window of the house in the centre at the top. As the only figure capable of seeing all the activity, it is a stand-in for us as viewers. With this theatre prop the actual and the fictional worlds of Carnival blend together. When it is burned the utopia ends and austere Lent begins.

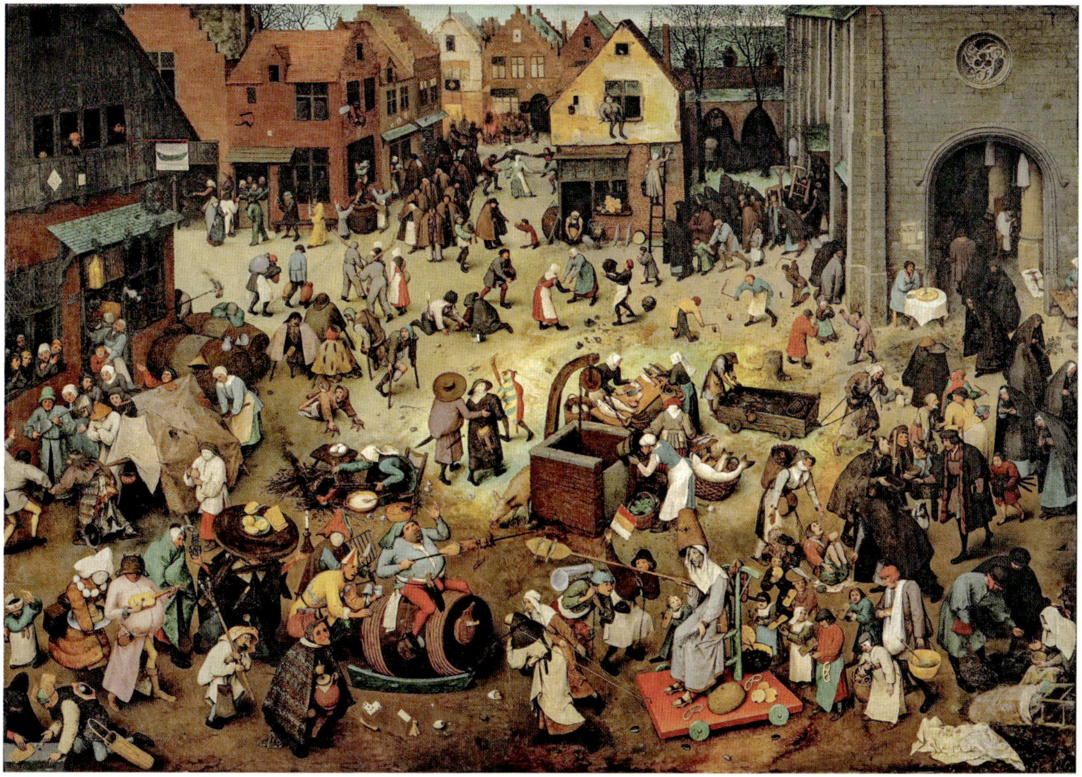

The Rabbit Hunt, 1560

Etching
22.3 × 19.1 cm
Staatliche Museen zu Berlin, Kupferstichkabinett

This etching is unique in that it is the single known work that Bruegel not only drew but also engraved himself. And the fact that he was not so practised in this metier as the engravers who normally transferred his drawings can be seen (with a magnifying glass) on the left at the very bottom next to his signature, where he engraved the date 1560 backwards, so that it appears reversed on the print. A simple mistake that can be ascribed to his lack of engraving experience. Otherwise the print only seems somewhat less precise than those of his colleagues, who transferred his drawings with great accuracy. His own work more closely resembles his drawing style with dots and short strokes, which he drew and scribed on the plate with different pressures. We see a typical Bruegel landscape; from an undefined elevation one can see next to a tree the activity that gives the print its name: a rabbit hunt. A hunter accompanied by his scruffy dog is aiming his crossbow at one of three rabbits nibbling in the grass a few metres away. The tree leads the eye back to the hill topped by a castle. Above it stands the signature of Bruegel's publisher of the print, "H. Cock". In the direction the crossbow is pointing the landscape expands across an orchard and a pair of houses, above a meandering river on which two ships are sailing towards the distant city and behind which lies the ocean. The wealth of detail and the precision of his depiction are astonishing even in this early work: the houses are from one to two centimetres tall, and the church tower in the coastal city reaches a height of scarcely five millimetres—yet everything is clear and readily recognisable. Also the curious scene taking place in the foreground: for while the hunter aims at the rabbit with his crossbow another man with a pike is sneaking towards him from behind the tree—we cannot know why. An explanation is perhaps provided by an aphorism found in the ancient writer Terence's play *Eunuchus*: "You search for game and are yourself the rabbit". The play was very well known in Bruegel's time and even used as a text in schools and the proverb was also quoted in Erasmus's *Adagia*, so Bruegel's engraving was readily understood, which probably contributed to its success. Being on guard, as is here recommended, was an important precaution in the Netherlands at that time, one that could sometimes prolong a person's life.

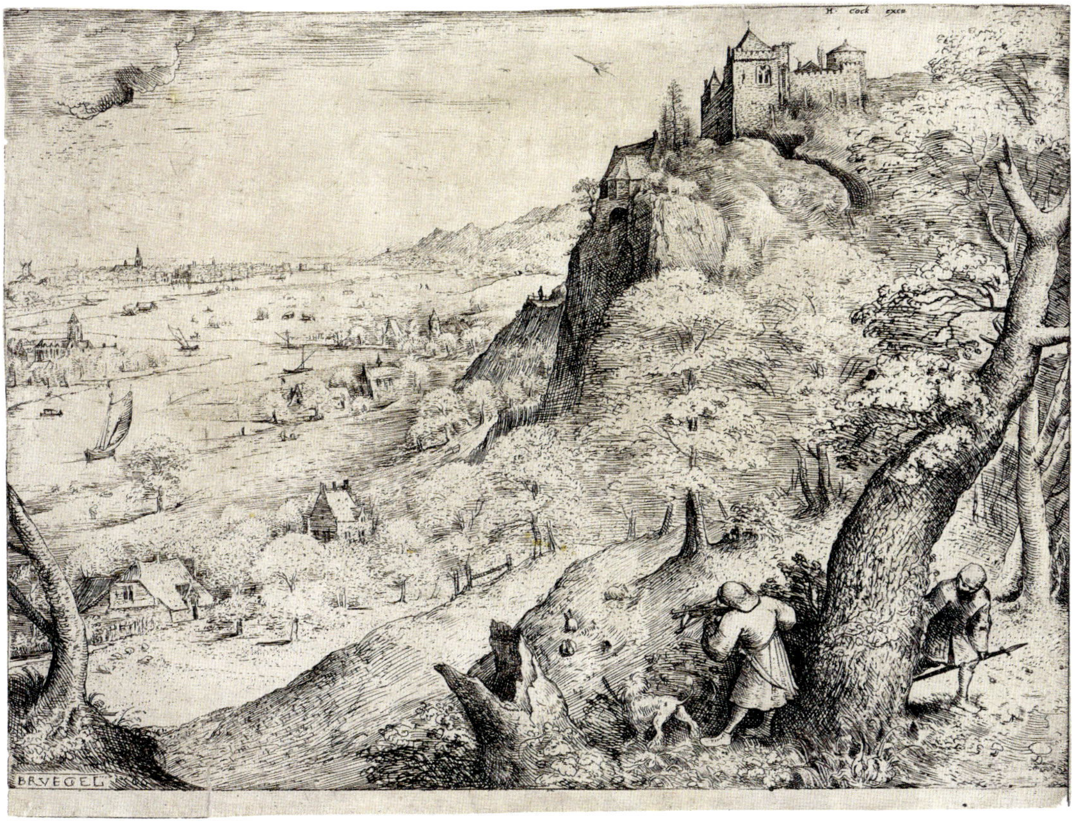
H. cock exc
BRVEGEL

Armed Three-Master on the Open Sea Accompanied by a Galley, 1561/62

Engraving by Frans Huys
33.6 × 26 cm
The Metropolitan Museum of Art, New York

After Charles V died in 1558 a huge model of a "navis victoria", a triumphal ship, was drawn through the streets during the obsequies. Hieronymus Cock subsequently had his drawing of it published by the Christoph Plantin firm in 1559, doubtless with great success. Navigation naturally played a hugely important role in the Netherlands, for it was the source of the country's wealth; discoveries, conquests and trade were unthinkable without it. Bruegel apparently had a particular interest in navigation, as we see time and again from the depictions of ships along the coasts in his landscapes. It is highly probable that he also drew ships on his Italian journey, as in 1561 he published at Cock's the engraving *Naval Battle in the Strait of Messina* (page 13), which is certain to have been based on his own observations and sketches. Attacks by Turkish pirates in the Messina and Reggio region were frequent in his time. From these two prints it is possible that Bruegel and Cock got the idea for a graphic series, so Bruegel drew a full ten views of various common types of ships at the time: trading and coastal vessels like buoys, masted galleys and schooners, the most common type of ship in the fifteenth and sixteenth centuries. They could be outfitted for either trading or combat. For this series Bruegel drew designs, none of which survive, in meticulous detail, but this does not mean that they are truthful images of either the ships or the scenery. He worked here the same way he did in his landscape drawings: views and details were composed for artistic purposes, so that the pictures seem realistic but not necessarily factual: despite their billowing sails, both of these ships are barely listing, they remain upright in the water in spite of the indicated windy conditions. If the three-master were to tip in response to such a gale it would probably sink, because through the gunports, the openings for the cannons, it would take on too much water. In any case, Bruegel drew them too close to the waterline and on a peaceful voyage, as here, they would have been closed and thus considerably less impressive visually. To many of the prints in the series Bruegel, the publisher or the engraver added mythological scenes like the fall of Icarus or that of Phaethon with the sun chariot of his father Helios. The series appears to have been successful, for it was continued until 1565.

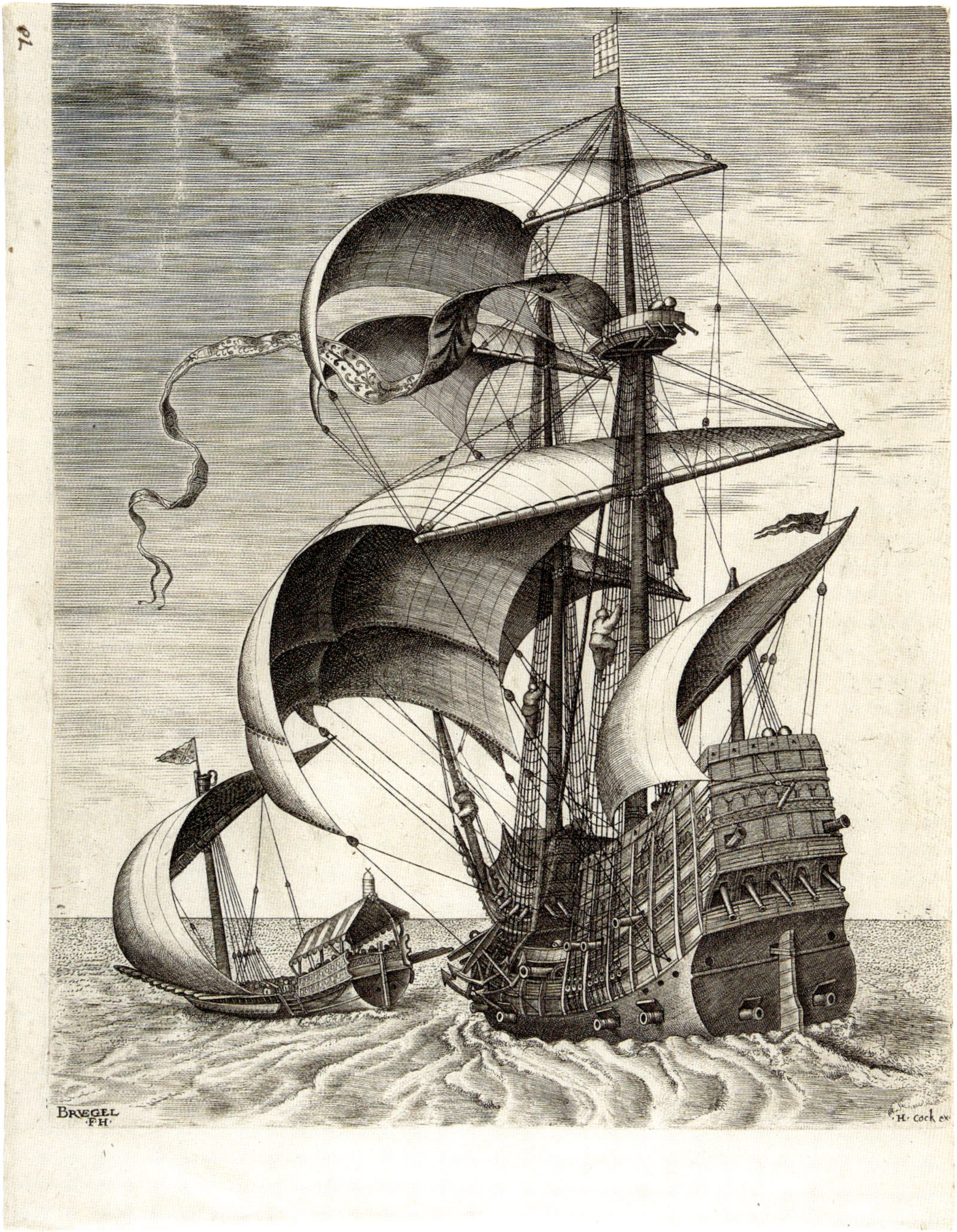
BRVEGEL
·F·H·
H· cock ex·

The Fall of the Rebel Angels, 1562

Oil on oak panel
117 × 162 cm
Musées royaux des Beaux-Arts de Belgique, Brussels

Bruegel told of the beginning and the end of time. Occasioned by the separation of light from darkness (Genesis 1:4), a battle of angels broke out led by Michael and Lucifer. Lucifer was cast out, because he wanted to place himself on the same level as God. In his fall he tore other rebel angels with him. Lucifer became God's adversary, the initiator of evil henceforth equated with Satan. In the Apocalypse (Revelation 12), Michael fights with him at the end of time in a final battle between good and evil. The painting is divided horizontally into two halves: the world and hell at the bottom, a radiantly lit heaven at the top. Out of the latter Lucifer's angels are tumbling like a plague of locusts and in their downward course are turned into diabolical monsters. They are thrust into hell by Michael and his host of angels bearing trumpets and swords. The archangel himself fights with the dragon "having seven heads . . . and on his heads seven diadems" (Revelation 12:3): "and that great dragon was cast out, that old serpent, who is called the devil and Satan, who seduceth the whole world; and he was cast unto the earth, and his angels were thrown down with him" (Revelation 12:9). Bruegel combines these events and has the roiling battle extend beyond the picture's edges, thereby interpreting the fight as omnipresent and eternal. In the painter's depiction of the fall of the dragon and his retinue most of the figures are seen to be falling backwards with arms and legs thrust upwards—first of all the dragon, at least four of whose seven heads can be seen with their diadems. As sources for his demonic world of fantastic hybrid creatures Bruegel used collections of Indian art and exotic New World animals which he was able to study in Antwerp's cabinets of curiosities. From various plants to butterflies, the sloth and the armadillo whose carapace here mutates into the armour of a falling angel, to the shiny and slippery bodies of the lizard- and fish-like creatures, the painting is a masterpiece of nature observation and pictorial density. In the centre the light-footed archangel is standing on the belly of the dragon in golden armour and with his sword. Like the other angels, he is somewhat elongated. Whereas this picture subject was used by painters trained in Italy as a chance to depict ideal, athletic bodies, Bruegel quite deliberately drew on earlier Netherlandish art, clearly rejecting the Renaissance style in the depiction of figures. Thus it is even possible that the red turban beneath Michael's feet was meant as an homage to Jan van Eyck and his self-portrait from 1433.

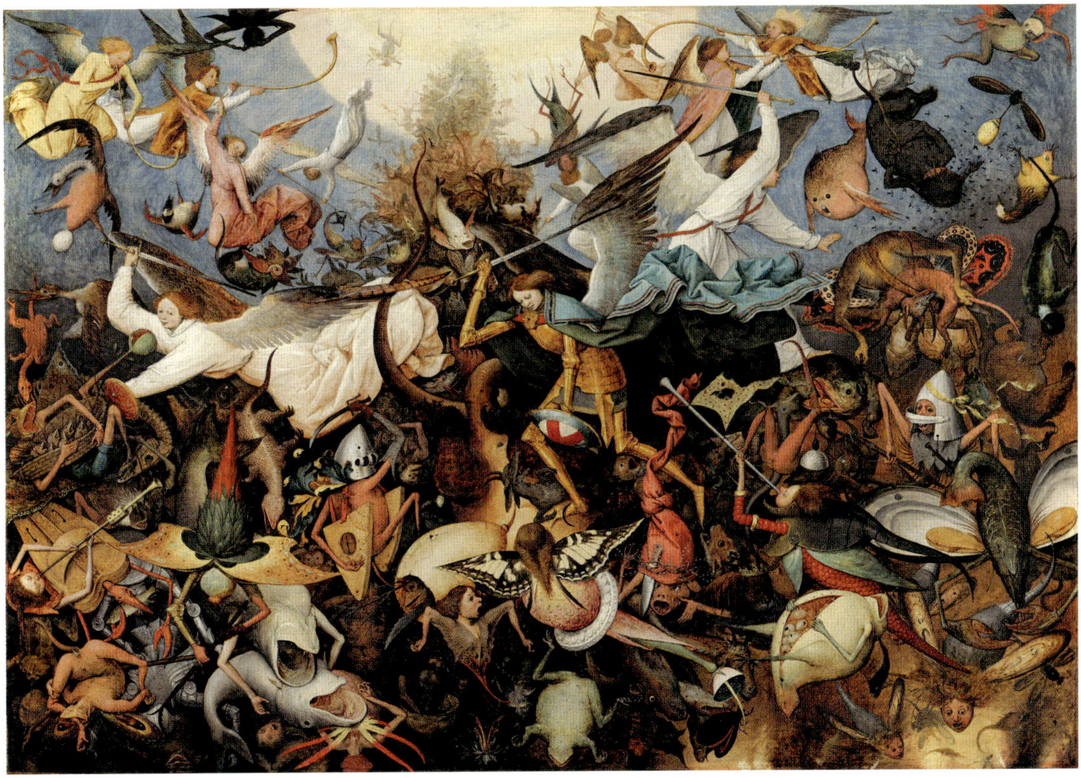

The Triumph of Death, 1562/63

Oil on oak panel
117 × 162 cm
Prado, Madrid

In a desolate world armies of the dead are killing the last people in a kind of final battle. The end is heralded on the left. The skeleton next to the clock on the round structure below shows there is only one thing left: death. No one is spared: his wealth is no help to the king, their faith no aid to the cardinal and pilgrim, their courage no advantage to the lansquenets. Noble ladies are in shock because they see only now that it is death that has called them to table. Perhaps they were deceived by the skeleton with the lifelike mask that is pouring chilled wine. A couple in front of the table think they can save themselves through love but fail to notice that behind them Death has already started singing their last verse. And the fool believes that he can hide from Death. It is a merciless and unemotional massacre in which neither children nor animals are spared. Death strikes all: every age, each sex, every class, every skin colour, every religion. Whereas up until now Death had at least a positive aspect in that a person exits the sinful world in favour of a possible paradisical hereafter, here there is no longer such hope: Death is invariably brutal and he comes suddenly—no time for repentance. And he is final—no redemption. The surviving people are being herded by the scythe-wielding horseman of the Apocalypse into a kind of trap in the form of a gigantic coffin and return as an army of the dead. At least until Death alone remains. It is the people themselves who kill each other. Bruegel's frighteningly fascinating painting of slaughter is like an encyclopaedia of killing, with one exception: no one is being crucified. Even Christ is no longer present as a last glimmer of hope. Hell appears merely as a theatre prop, a burning cart, an infernal machine driven by a pair of Bosch figures. The world is going up in flames and life is disappearing. Death here is real. The theological sources for such thinking were very probably the writings of Sebastian Franck (page 24), according to which there is no Last Judgement, only an end time—and here it has begun. Merely a single skeleton appears to have fallen into melancholic reflection upon seeing a dead bird floating in the water—but possibly this is only a mean, ironic switch on Bruegel's part. Such total hopelessness was entirely new in art. At whose behest is Death at work? And at whose behest Bruegel? Who would have bought or commissioned such a work? There are no records of the whereabouts of this extraordinary picture during Bruegel's lifetime.

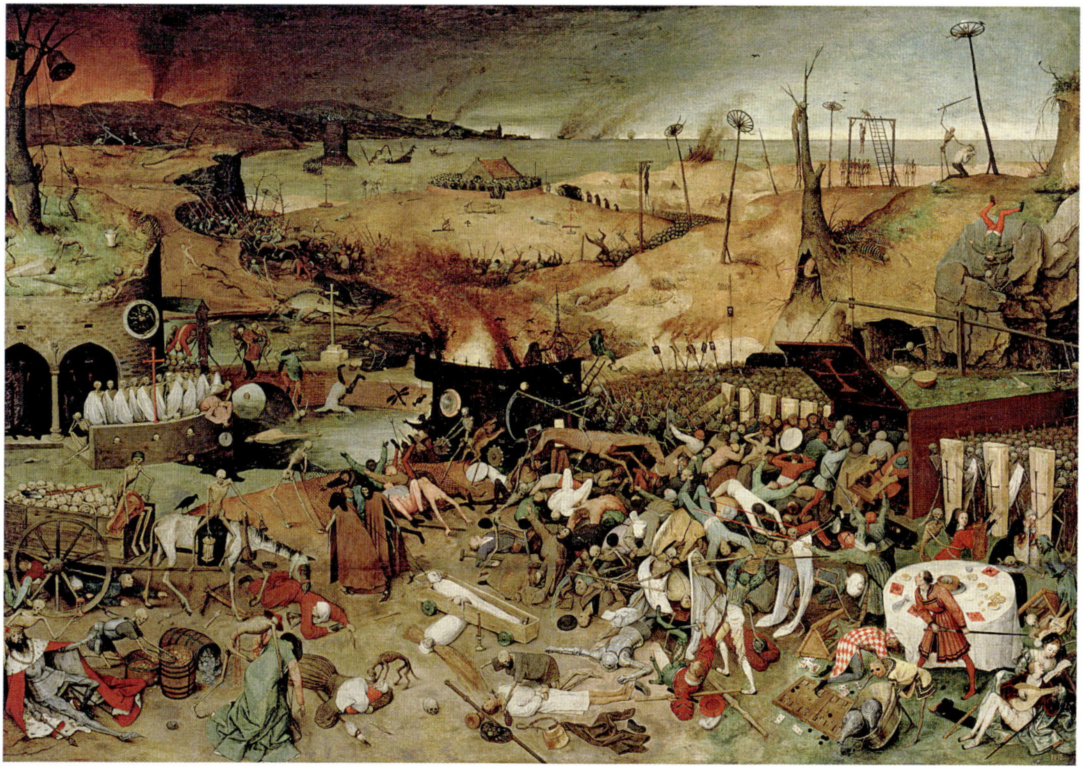

The Adoration of the Magi in the Snow, 1563

Oil on oak panel
35 × 55 cm
Oskar Reinhart collection 'Am Römerholz', Winterthur

The Adoration of the Magi in the Snow is the first of five snowy pictures of Bruegel's and the only one in which the snow is still falling. The effect is very impressive, for as a viewer one knows that the flakes are all painted on the picture surface but nevertheless succumbs to the illusion that it is snowing just as hard in the depth of the picture, or far back in the village. Bruegel's picture is not the first one to show falling snow. It is possible that on his Italian trip he visited the Palazzo Pubblico in Siena, already famous at the time, in which Ambrogio Lorenzetti (c. 1290–1348) painted the first snowfall in art history between 1337 and 1339. Among his seasonal pictures winter appears as a man in a cloak and hat in driving snow holding a snowball in his hand, apparently undecided what to do with it. It is very possible that this inspired Bruegel to actually translate visual experience into pictures. The atmosphere created by the falling snow together with typical winter light veils the true subject matter, the Adoration of the Kings, which is under way at the far left, almost unnoticed by the villagers. At the time it was created Mary was more prominent, as her cloak was painted with the blue pigment smalt which has changed over time into a beige-brown. Two of the three kings are kneeling before her while the third waits his turn. A few metres back is their retinue with pack animals. The villagers are bundled up in their warmest clothes and appear to want to get back to their snug chambers as fast as possible. The large derelict building on the right side is supported by a long pole which does not seem especially reassuring given the building's size. This may be an allusion to the end of the Old Covenant, which is now being renewed by the birth of Christ. Beneath the snow-covered awning stretched between the palace and the village pond a makeshift bar has been set up which calls attention to itself with the tankard hung out as a sign. Wood next to the wall stands ready for a warming fire. In the right foreground a child in his sled is heading towards a hole in the frozen pond from which men have been drawing water. Whether the child is an allusion to Christ's death or the imminent Massacre of the Innocents (page 87) is unclear. In any case, on closer inspection a relatively large number of soldiers with lances and swords appear to be approaching. At the very back one can see some of them behind a standing wheel. The painting was among Bruegel's most popular works even long after his death, for there are more than thirty copies of it by his son Pieter alone.

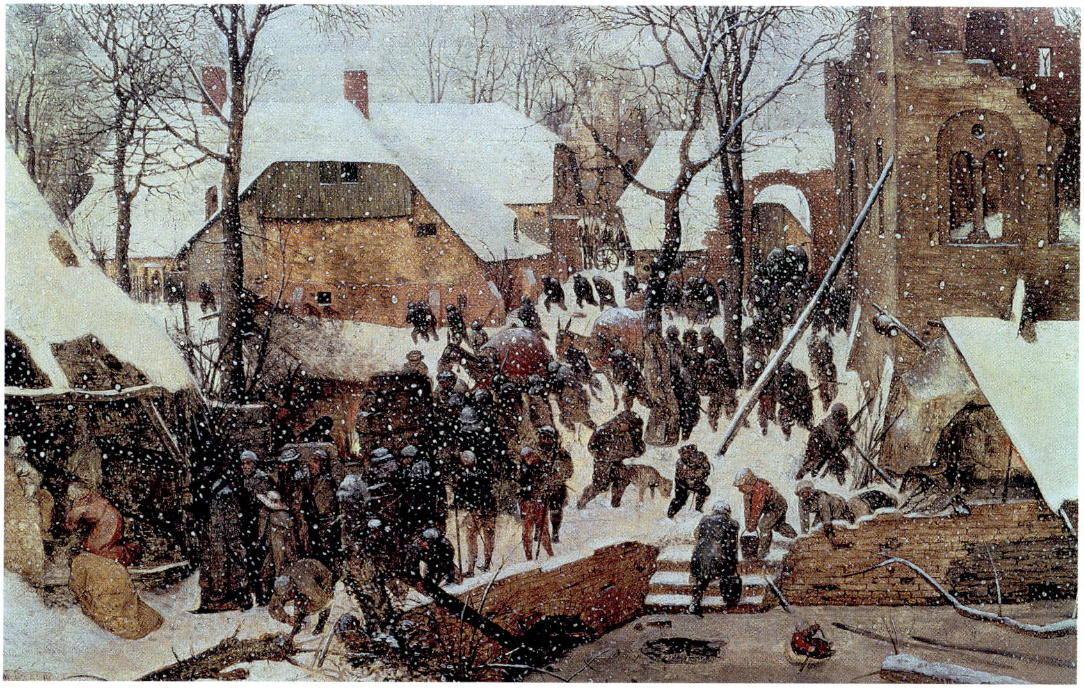

Two Monkeys, 1562

Oil on oak panel
19.9 × 23.3 cm
Staatliche Museen zu Berlin, Gemäldegalerie

In this unusually small picture, there is unusually little to see. In a stone window embrasure sit two monkeys chained to a thick ring. The opening provides a view of Antwerp and its harbour. There is considerable ship traffic on the Schelde, above which two birds are circling. The composition plays with the contrast between near and far: the embrasure is seen close up, at the same time serving as a frame for the expansive view of the city. It suggests a wide, open world and is a transit point for goods and cultures as well as for the fauna and flora of the world beyond the oceans. The monkeys, like so much else, numbered among the exotic sights to be marvelled at in the city. The two mangabeys were captured in the vastness of West Africa and now spend their lives chained in a drafty stone window niche in a northern European city. Their gazes and their poses have lost their vitality. As in his renderings of people, Bruegel also managed to express the monkeys' feelings in their poses. In fifteenth-century art theory the words "ars simia naturae" were often discussed: art mimics nature—just as monkeys mimic people, the artist mimics nature, "art is the monkey of nature". In this sense one can associate the monkeys with Bruegel, an association strengthened by the artist's signature directly below the animal on the left. Bruegel perhaps used the exotic creatures in order to instigate a debate about freedom and the freedom of art: painting was embattled by Protestants on the one hand and on the other Protestants and the Netherlanders as a whole were harassed by the Spanish, which Bruegel appears to criticise relatively openly in many of his pictures. The degree to which his humanist acquaintances around Abraham Ortelius and Niclaes Jongelinck or the influential art collector Cardinal Grandvelle protectively shielded him is unknown. This picture can be read as a subtle indication of the inner freedom of an artist who realises freedom in his imagination which one can see symbolised by the two circling birds. Thus Psalm 123:7 applies: "Our soul hath been delivered as a sparrow out of the snare of the fowlers. The snare is broken, and we are delivered".

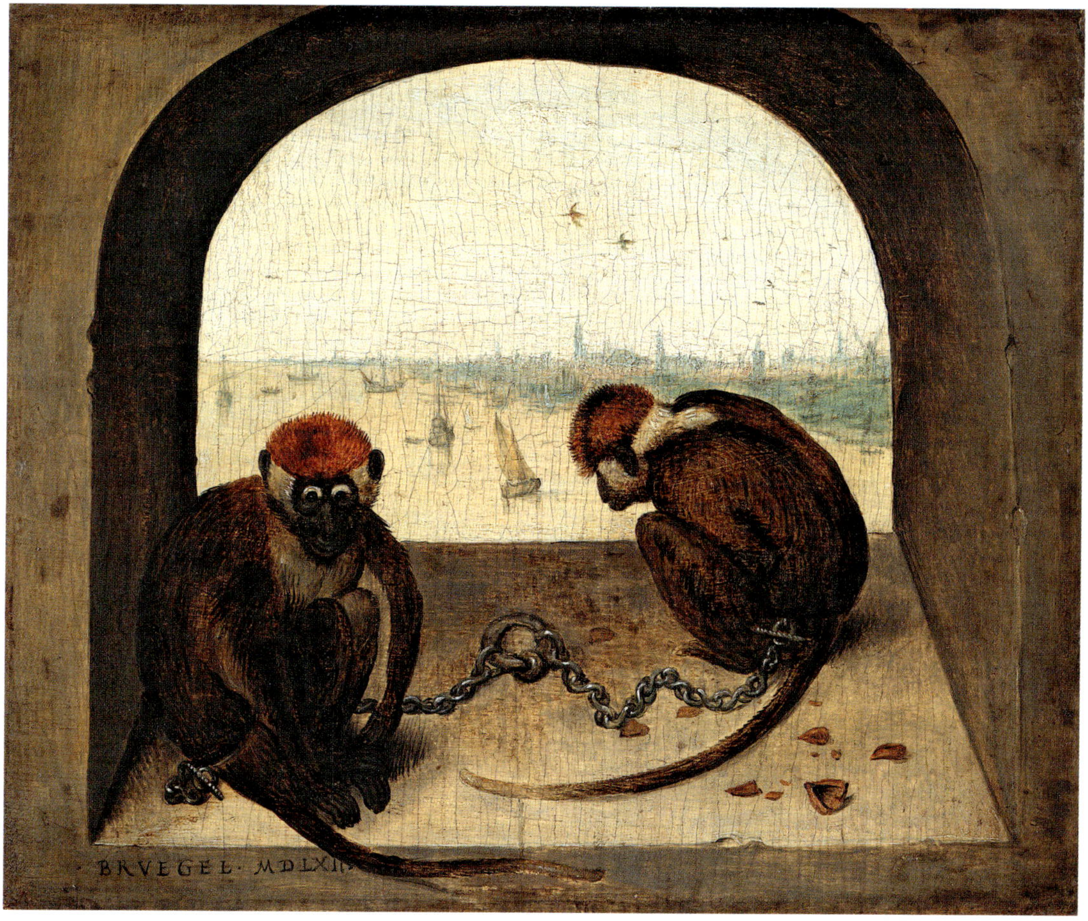
BRVEGEL · MDLXII

Mad Meg, 1563

Oil on wood
116.4 × 162.1 cm
Museum Mayer van den Bergh, Antwerp

Hell is burning and the world appears to be sinking into chaos. On a rise in the foreground a woman armed with a sword and protected by a helmet, armour and glove is racing towards hell. "Dulle Griet" or Mad Meg, is a figure from the world of Netherlandish saga. She is a Flemish shrew, a goddess of vengeance whose boldness is legendary. She fears neither Death nor the devil. As it is said in the vernacular, she plunders before the gates of hell and is capable of returning unharmed from a raid on the underworld. She apparently has a part of this plunder behind her already in view of her booty. With her left arm she carries a stuffed sack, a basket with a pan and household utensils as well as a hoop-handled bowl filled with gold and silver objects. Under her arm she also clutches a casket that is presumably filled with coins. She now appears to be engaged in her next caper as she is heading straight towards the jaws of hell. The remaining small monsters along her way will not detain her, especially since many of them gaze at her in fear. On the bridge behind Mad Meg a mob of furious women are fighting with smaller and larger monsters and snatching up whatever there is to snatch. On the gable of a house sits a male creature balancing a boat on his head and "scooping money out of his own behind" that the women below are collecting. The year 1563, around the time this painting was made, was a turning point for Bruegel: among the few assured dates in his life are his marriage to Mayken Coecke and the move to Brussels connected with it. They both took place in 1563. It seems as if this work is an artistic closure with the world of Hieronymus Bosch. Bruegel here enters into the figural world of his famous predecessor and revives its hell and its monsters. The imaginativeness and the entire arrangement of the somewhat chaotic-seeming painting are impressive: hellfire glows across the whole width of the picture from yellow to black, while the foreground is limited to a dull brown. The world outside hell is by no means beautiful. And it appears that it can no longer be explained and understood through reason. Bruegel is here very close to Bosch and his visions of hell; but he also seems to have surmounted them in that he no longer lends his monsters anything diabolical or supernatural. He makes fun of Mad Meg and her cohort. In this respect Bruegel is like Mad Meg himself: he plunders the hell (of Bosch) and comes back from it unscathed.

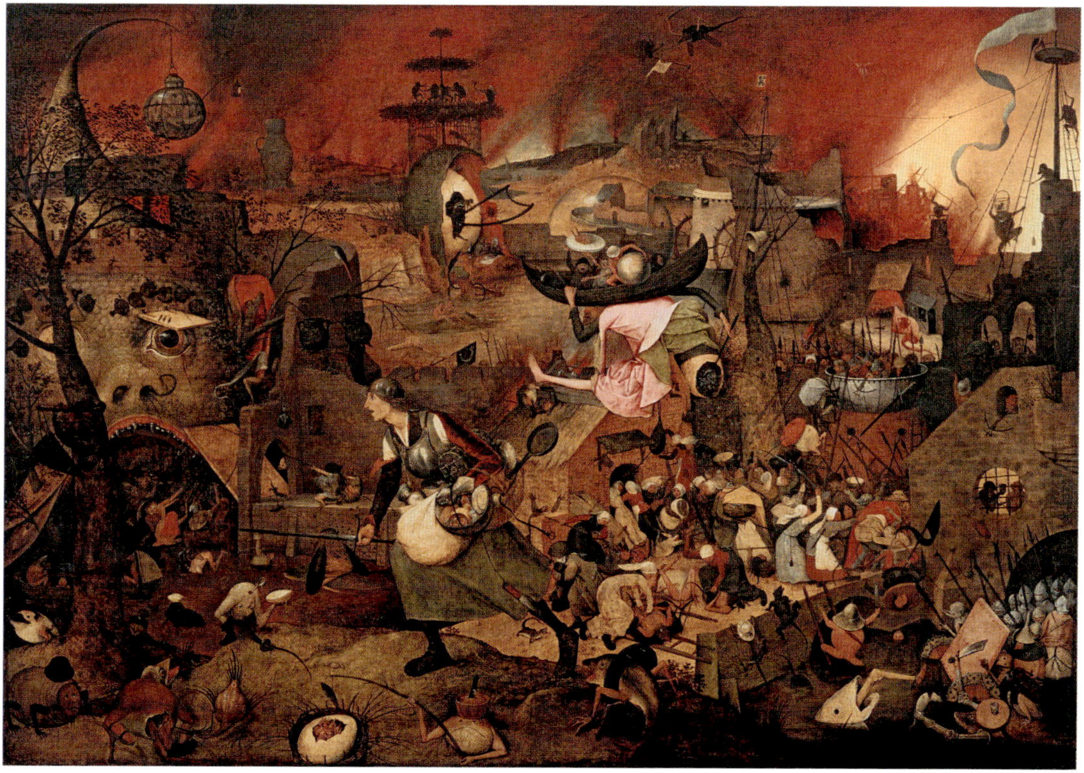

The Tower of Babel, 1563

Oil on oak panel
114.3 × 155.1 cm
Kunsthistorisches Museum, Vienna

The Tower of Babel, c. 1565 page 71

Oil on oak panel
59.9 × 74.6 cm
Museum Boijmans Van Beuningen, Rotterdam

The Tower of Babel is a story of ambition, communal will, jealousy and failure owing to miscommunication. In Genesis the people said: "Come, let us make a city and a tower; the top whereof may reach to heaven: and let us make our name famous before we be scattered abroad into all lands" (Genesis 11:4). And so they did. They built their city on the coast, one that was definitely planned for expansion, as one can see in the Vienna picture. In addition they erected an incredibly tall tower. Bruegel shows the ruler Nimrod visiting the building site, something not mentioned in the Bible. Stonemasons kneel before him in greeting. The monumental structure towers into the sky and on the left side appears to be virtually finished. From the tiny figures on the building one derives a sense of its enormous size. Yet the people and their activities are clearly visible: a number of the arcades are already inhabited—a Bruegel innovation. We see women seated together, laundry hanging across railings, horse-drawn carts delivering vegetables, chickens being fed while construction continues. Everything seems relaxed. Men are taking a break on the meadow between Nimrod and the tower and to the left of them tools and such like are being forged in smithies. The city itself is so densely built up that one can only imagine what so many people might be up to. Work on the tower appears to be not so far advanced on the right side, especially since portions of rock are projecting or have to be built around. Since the Middle Ages the subject of the Tower of Babel had given artists a chance to illustrate contemporary building techniques. Bruegel does so in both works in great detail. We see all sorts of cranes and hoists, masonry and plasterwork, stonecutting, scaffolding and the delivery on wagons and ships of all the necessary building materials from wood to bricks as well as foodstuffs. At the open spots we can see the centring for the arches, parts of the interior construction and scaffolding for the facade work. It is a huge building site involving the whole city, occupying the entire population, yet apparently peaceful. Whereas the Vienna picture employs bright colours and seems almost idyllic, in the

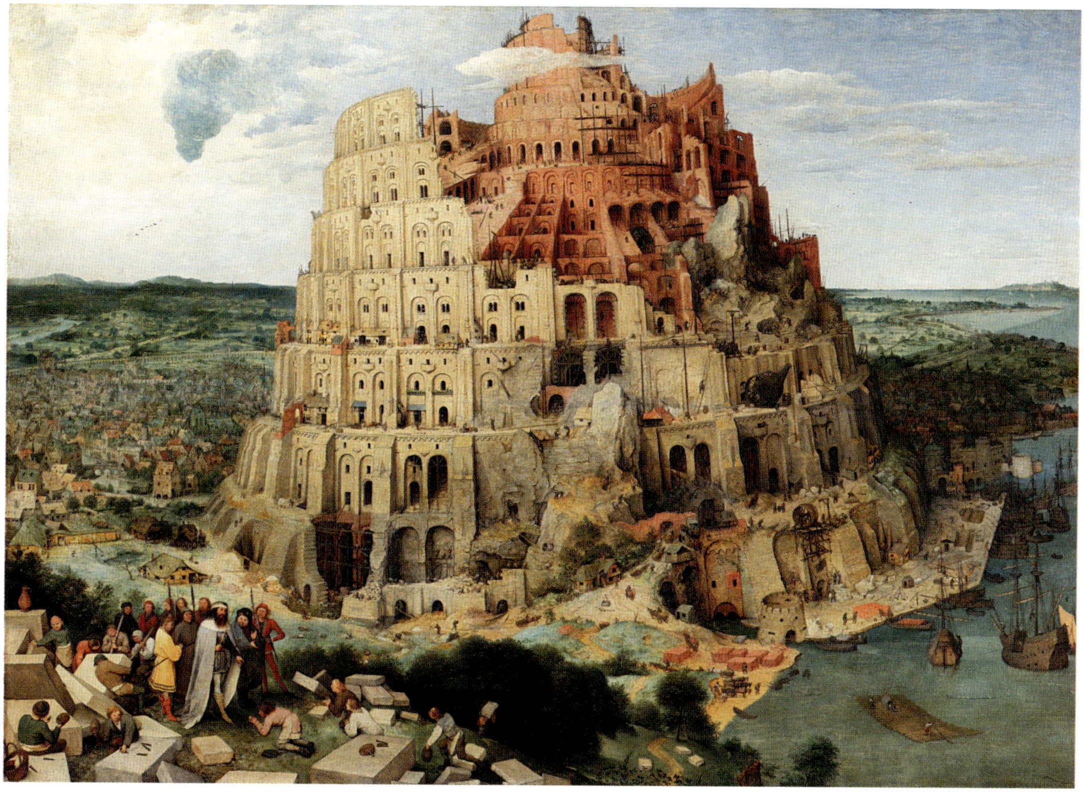

version completed some two years later the sky is darkening. This picture is only roughly half as large, but here the tower rises up above the clouds and, based on the size of the figures, is some two and a half times the size of the "Vienna tower". And it is nearly completed. In the Rotterdam picture the city is barely visible. Instead, we see a landscape dotted with a few houses, everybody has already moved into the tower. Only a few are still living along the access roads and next to the harbour. Here too there is much building activity: on the left bricks and lime are being delivered which Bruegel emphasises with the coloured walls in red and white. The terraces winding upward around the tower are as wide as streets and similarly bustling. Halfway up some kind of a procession is in progress complete with a red baldachin. If one looks into the open arcades—all of them individually designed, some resembling church portals, some the facades of houses—one gets a sense, thanks to Bruegel's amazing painterly skill, of the depth of the enormous structure. Both paintings are grandiose in their love of detail and the rendering of the various stone surfaces. At the top of the structure one has a feel for its extremely complex construction and recognises that Bruegel patterned it after the colosseum in Rome which he knew very well from his own observation and from drawings and prints by his colleague Maarten van Heemskerck. Great harmony seems to prevail in both vertical cities and the people have come close to their goal of not being scattered abroad. "And the Lord came down to see the city and the tower, which the children of Adam were building. And he said: Behold, it is one people, and all have one tongue: and they have begun to do this, neither will they leave off from their designs, till they accomplish them in deed" (Genesis 11:5–6). And God was by no means pleased, for he felt threatened in his power and in jealousy drove a wedge into this community: "Come ye, therefore, let us go down and there confound their tongue, that they may not understand one another's speech. And so the Lord scattered them from that place into all lands, and they ceased to build the city" (Genesis 11:7–8). God did not destroy the tower, but he did destroy the community by taking away what they shared, their language, their ability to communicate. The human yearning for unity is shattered by the impossibility of a common language—something that seems strangely topical today. What is frequently declared as human arrogance in wishing to outdo God is perhaps more accurately a divine being's inability to tolerate others next to him, especially if they were created by him in his own image. Babel translates as (linguistic) confusion, something that was reflected in Bruegel's time as well. Not in the variety of languages and cultures heard and seen in Antwerp, but in religion. Here unity has been lost due to the Reformation and the many reform movements.

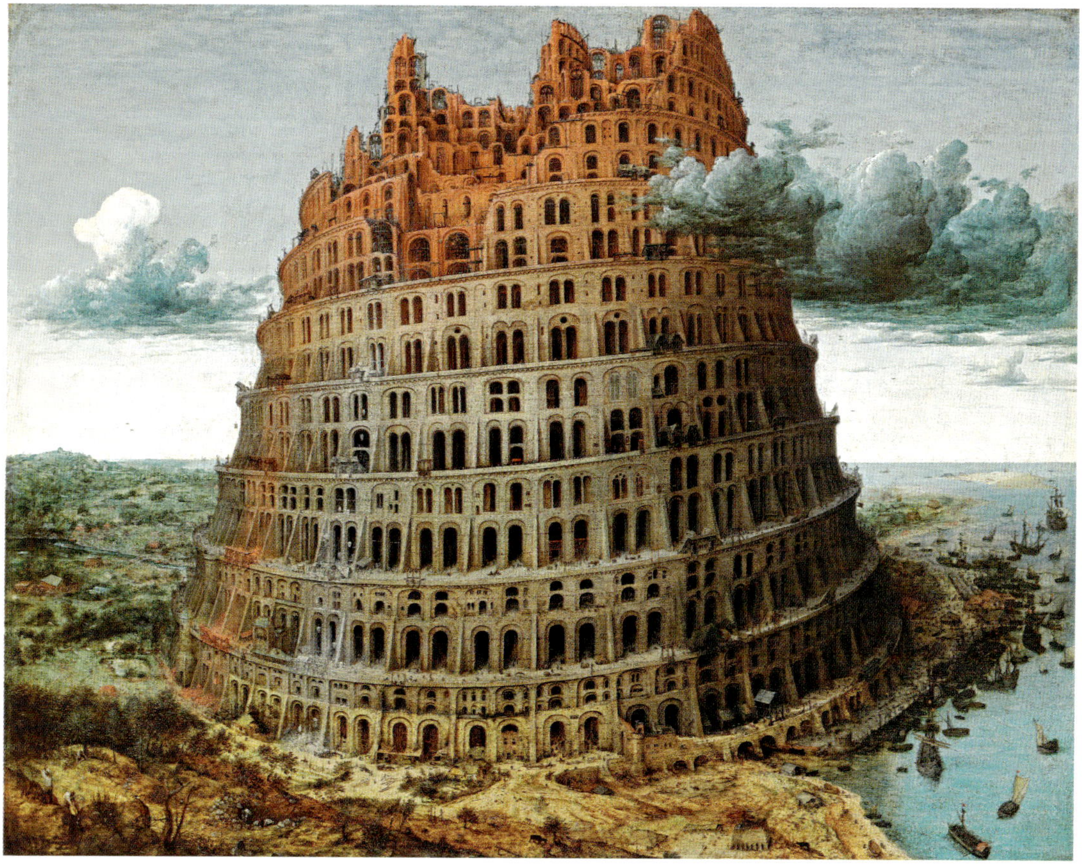

The Death of the Virgin, c. 1564

Oil on oak panel
67.7 × 85.3 cm
National Trust Collection, Upton House, Warwickshire

The Virgin's death was a favourite picture subject in the art of northern Europe. Martin Schongauer, Albrecht Dürer, Hugo van der Goes and others had engraved and painted their own versions of it before Bruegel created something completely new. Mary's death is not mentioned in the Bible; the story of it comes from the medieval *Golden Legend* by Jacobus de Voragine (c. 1228–1298). It relates that at the end of her life Mary begged to see the apostles once more and they were promptly borne in on clouds. In Bruegel's version he takes several very new approaches. He stages the scene as a dream of John's, who is seen asleep on a chair on the left, his hands folded in prayer. Bruegel also pictures the reunion for the first time as a nighttime scene. In a darkened room all of them have gathered around Mary's bed; Peter is handing her a candle, Mary Magdelene is plumping up her pillow and the others are praying. Mary sits upright, gazing at a crucifix lying on another pillow at the foot of the bed. The room is only sparsely lit. Next to John a fire is burning in the fireplace, in front of which a cat has made itself comfortable. On the shelf in the background stand two candles, another on the table illuminates the dishes left from a last shared meal and Peter holds a fourth candle. But the brightest light is a supernatural one, a wreath of rays emanating from Mary. This illumination is something of a pioneering feat artistically, for at this time nighttime pictures were still rare. One of the first was painted by Taddeo Gaddi (c. 1290–1366); Bruegel could possibly have seen it in Florence's Santa Croce. Another appears in the Limburg brothers' *Les Très Riches Heures*, painted between 1410 and 1416 for the Duc de Berry. The heyday of night pictures began only with the chiaroscuro painting of Caravaggio (1571–1610). Realist that he was, Bruegel used John's dream to explain Mary's heavenly radiance. It was Bruegel's friend Abraham Ortelius who commissioned this Catholic painting (there is no Mary worship in the Protestant Church). Whether one can conclude from it anything about Bruegel's own beliefs remains unclear. For Ortelius, however, it was an important work, because in 1574 he had it engraved by Philipp Galle "for him and his friends" to give away, with a text he wrote himself. The original was later acquired by Isabella Brant (1591–1626), the first wife of Peter Paul Rubens, who painted a copy of it.

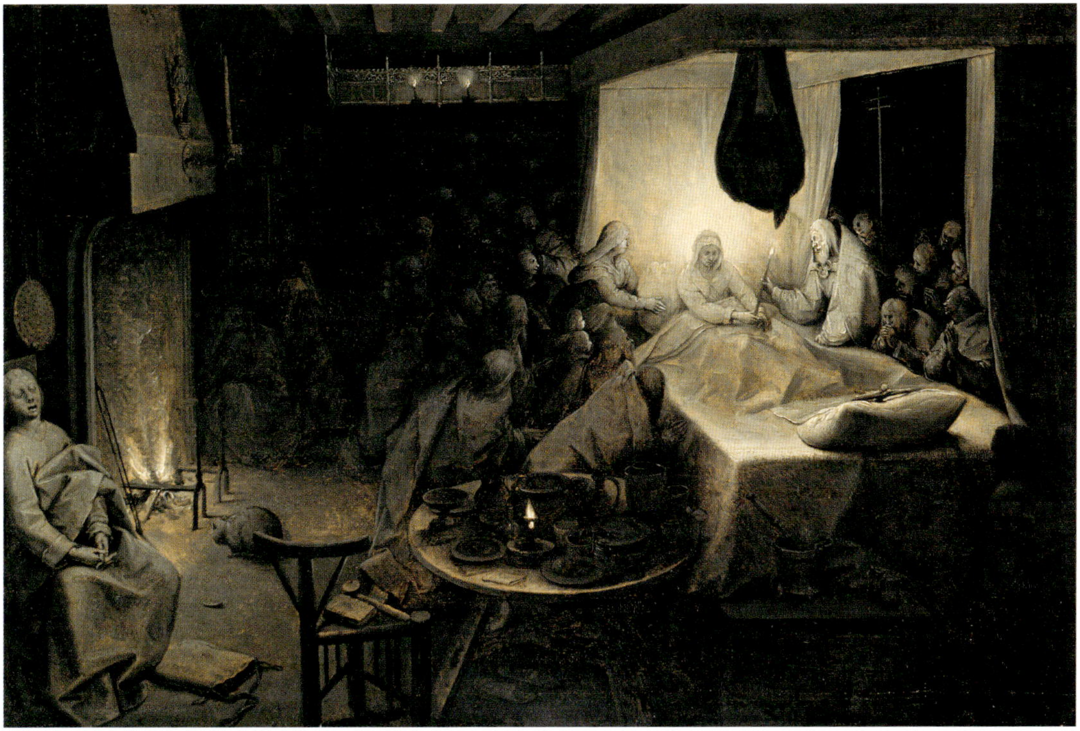

The Adoration of the Kings, 1564

Oil on oak panel
112.1 × 83.9 cm
National Gallery, London

Epiphany celebrates the discovery of Christ's incarnation. If driving snow made seeing and appreciating difficult for the viewer in the *Adoration* from 1563 (page 63), here Bruegel makes it no easier. It is questionable whether he even intended to. It is his only portrait-format painting and the only one from this period with large figures like those that appear in Italian painting, but which had not yet featured in his previous work thus far. Given its format, it could be an altarpiece and votive picture but the depiction makes this doubtful. It seems more likely that Bruegel used the subject as an opportunity to think about the role of the votive picture itself—seeing and discovery are frequent subjects in his pictures. Caspar, the oldest king, has set his sceptre and beret aside and is kneeling before Jesus who appears to be drawing back. He is extending a vessel filled with myrrh but is quite obviously looking past the infant in the direction of the stall. To his left Melchior is starting to kneel with his chalice but gazes at Caspar in turn. The black Balthasar also fails to look at the child as he seems to be fixed on something outside the picture. Non-seeing often implies non-understanding in Bruegel, non-knowing, thus one has to ask whether the "three wise men from the east" truly grasp what is taking place before their eyes. Bruegel has emphasised this possible ignorance with the satirical getup of the two kings on the left: Melchior is tousled with stringy hair and Caspar's clothing is strangely inappropriate: the pink coat is much too short, while the sleeves are absurdly long. And, if he were to put his hat back on his much too small head, he would completely disappear beneath it. Non-recognition continues in the soldiers who in terms of iconography have no business being here in any case: they either only have eyes for the precious gifts or gape around in bewilderment. They too fail to look at Jesus, so do not acknowledge him as the Son of God. Is Bruegel here already introducing the soldiers who will later torture Jesus in his Passion? The man wearing glasses is also staring open-mouthed at the precious chalice. He will appear again a year later in Bruegel's drawing *Painter and Connoisseur* (page 34). For good measure a man has taken Joseph aside and is whispering something in his ear: is it about his paternity? The hat in front of Joseph's groin would appear to suggest as much. The only figure who is not pictured satirically is the nobleman with a beard and dark clothing. He seems to be observing the scene with disillusionment. Perhaps he is the picture's patron with whom Bruegel shared doubts about what meaning and function the votive picture might still have in times of such turbulence in religion and politics.

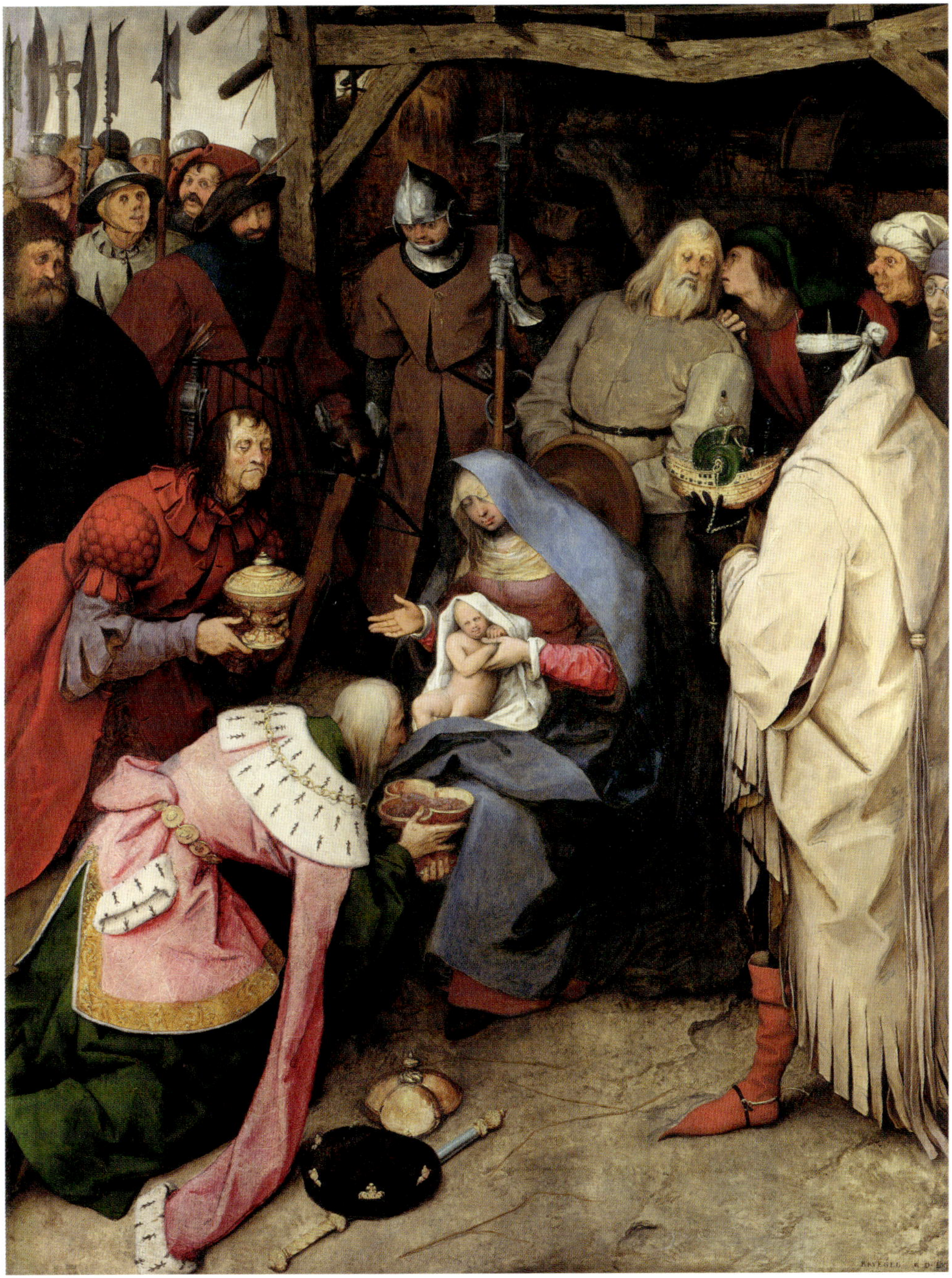

The Way to Calvary, 1564

Oil on oak panel
124.2 × 179.7 cm
Kunsthistorisches Museum, Vienna

Some 500 people are making their way up to Calvary from Jerusalem in order to witness an execution. On the far right a man stands in a white smock and red cap; this is Bruegel, planting himself in the picture as an onlooker. He is gazing directly into the centre where Jesus, almost unnoticed, has collapsed beneath the cross. In front of this a passage opens up at the left end of which two soldiers are trying to force a man, Simon of Cyrene, to take up the cross for Jesus (Mark 15:21). His wife, who holds a rosary and is obviously very pious, is trying to prevent it. It appears as if piety doesn't count if it costs something. On a rocky outcropping a group with Mary and John is mourning. It functions as a picture within a picture and is in no way related to what is taking place behind it. The figures already wear historical clothing and are painted in the style of Rogier van der Weyden (c. 1399–1464). The task of a lamentation group is to rouse *compassio*, the sympathy of the faithful, which in the actual picture narrative is nowhere to be seen. The fact that Jesus Christ is about to be executed "here and now" is of no particular interest. Instead, the people seem to have been drawn here by the simple amusement of an execution. And the fact that such spectacles are frequent is clear from the deep wheel ruts, the blood-soaked ground strewn with bones and skulls and finally the gallows and wheels on which corpses are still hanging and lying. With these the Jewish execution site Golgotha becomes a very contemporary place of execution for the Spanish Inquisition. Together with the Walloon-Spanish policemen in red coats and a Habsburg flag, in Bruegel's picture it is the Inquisition that becomes Christ's executioner, leading him and the two thieves to the execution site with twenty horsemen. And as is related in the Bible the sky above the flourishing landscape on the left grows darker over the gloomier wasteland on the right. The composition of this largest landscape painting of its time describes a circular movement proceeding across the entire picture, centred on the crag topped by a windmill. Bruegel reinforces this circular movement with the many wheels and the circle of people waiting at the actual crucifixion site. For him the wheel, like the mill on the rock, stands for eternal return, which Sebastian Franck describes thus: "And if it were to happen that Christ came again in his body . . . we would crucify him again. The world is always the same . . ., so that what was today will never be and recur tomorrow". In this sense one can also understand the lamentation group which has already experienced the death of Christ that is not yet shown in the picture. Past, present and future are dissolved.

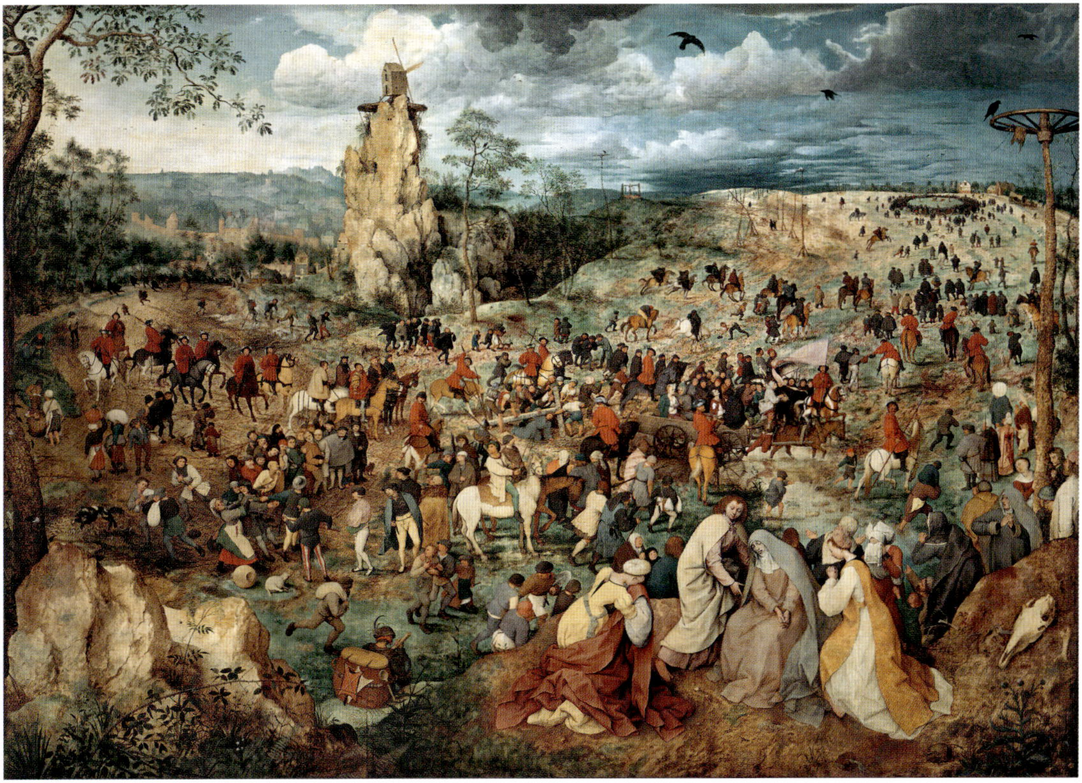

Winter Landscape with Skaters and Bird Trap, 1565

Oil on oak panel
37 × 55.5 cm
Musées royaux des Beaux-Arts de Belgique, Brussels

This work, about which we know neither who commissioned it nor who purchased it, was posthumously one of Bruegel's most successful. At least 127 copies are known, so that for a long time it was uncertain which one was the original. What made it so popular? As in other paintings, Bruegel captured an atmosphere with great sensitivity, that of a late afternoon under hazy winter clouds. The sky glows in a golden yellow and is reflected in the icy surface of the frozen river so that paradoxically the ice seems warmer and more inviting than the white snow. We are looking down on a contemplative village outside the gates of a city, probably Antwerp. It lines both sides of a small river and is connected by a bridge in the background. Children and grownups are enjoying themselves with all sorts of games on the ice. At roughly the height of the viewer a pair of bare bushes on a snow-covered slope in front of two houses can be seen on the right. A few birds have settled on them like the people on the river. And seemingly from a hiding place one can observe the bird trap, a simple device made out of a heavy wooden door, a small stick and a string. The latter is stretched taut up to a small hole in the wall of the first house behind which the trapper waits until as many birds as possible are trying to peck at the feed strewn beneath the door. The birds appear to be hopping cautiously around the trap, possibly warned by the magpie on the branch above or the rook in the tree in the upper right, which is cawing with an opened beak. As we see in *The Hunters in the Snow* (page 81), bird hunting offered a chance to slightly upgrade the meagre winter menu. The birds, which thanks to the trap live under the constant threat of danger, are like the people on the ice, who ignore the dangers of icy surfaces for the sake of the delightful lure of amusement. As we see in the near foreground, the ice is thin and a person could fall through it at any time. What accounted for the posthumous success of this work is difficult to say. Probably it was not so much the message of impending danger as simply the beauty of the winter countryside—at that time people were not so accustomed to seeing painted landscapes. And Bruegel's winter picture showed one in a loveliness never seen before. It definitely helped that it is a relatively small picture that could be copied quickly.

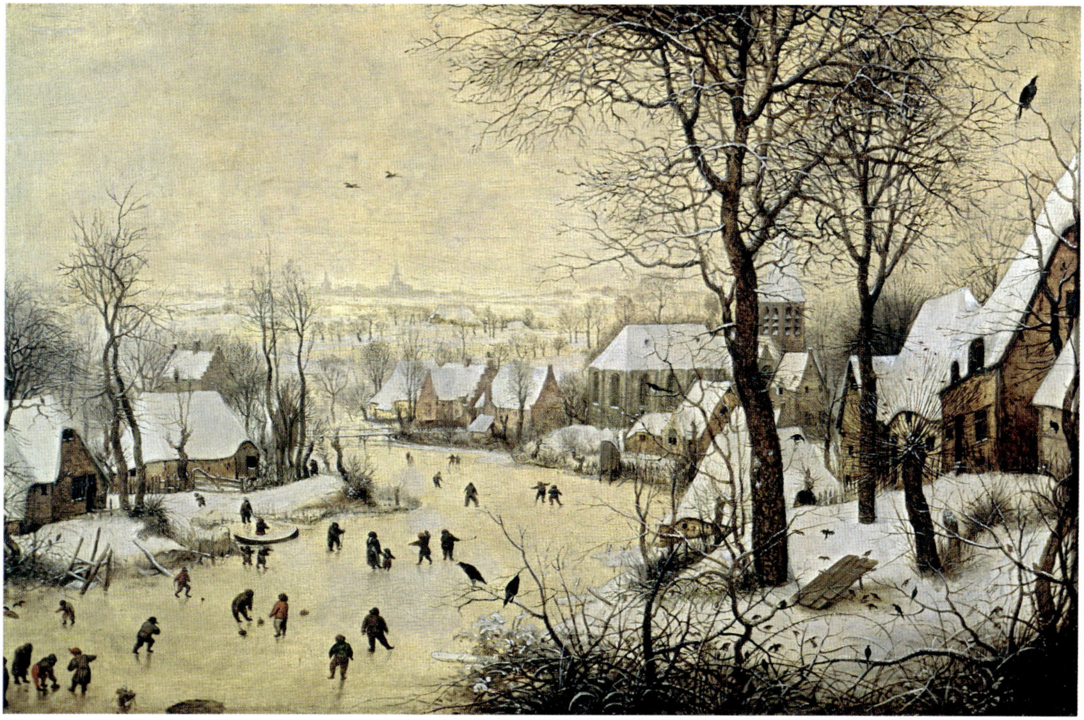

The Hunters in the Snow, 1565

Oil on oak panel
116.3 × 162.5 cm
Kunsthistorisches Museum, Vienna

The Hunters in the Snow is one of the world's most beloved paintings and a classic depiction of winter. And this even though it tells of poverty, hunger and the most bitter cold. Three hunters are returning from the hunt with their fourteen dogs and only a single fox as a prize. Ordinary people were not permitted to hunt more than small game; big game were a feudal privilege—one reason why we see bird traps time and again in Bruegel's winter pictures. With their meagre booty the men, bent over, are tramping their way through deep snow and even the dogs look exhausted and frustrated. One of them seems to be gazing out at the viewer, as if he could somehow make things easier. The row of four tall trees, whose bare branches create an impressive graphic pattern, lead one's gaze diagonally into the picture's depth. The hunters are heading in that direction, ignoring the inviting fire being stoked in front of the tavern on the left. The tavern "Dit is inden Hert" ("At the Hart") has seen better days, as one sees from its drooping sign. The fire is being used for singeing pig bristles, as winter is slaughtering time. From the rise a broad valley opens out to the hunters extending across several frozen village ponds to a jagged mountain spur and, on the left, as far as the coast. Bruegel unifies the vastness of the landscape with his convincingly atmospheric colouring. The leaden, blue-green sky is reflected in the icy surfaces of the ponds and contrasts with the yellowish white of the snow-covered ground, structured by means of grey-brown trees and people. In Bruegel's cycle of the seasons people are as much a part of nature as animals and plants. As in the other pictures of the series, he manages to evoke the season not so much by way of activities as with the prevailing mood. In the years of the "little ice age" especially cold temperatures were the rule in northern Europe, the consequences of which were recorded in many Netherlandish winter pictures. And one can see how cold it must have been when looking through the trees towards the horizon and discovering people walking as well as a horse-drawn sleigh pulling out on the ice, for even the ocean has frozen over (detail, page 28). In the right foreground the miller has stopped working because the water wheel is frozen solid. On the ponds people are amusing themselves with skating and games. They fail to notice that not far behind the church a chimney has caught fire and neighbours are rushing up with ladders to help. Everything is happening at once and joy and sorrow are always close together, side by side. And even in the deepest cold it would not be a Bruegel painting without his trademark man taking a pee.

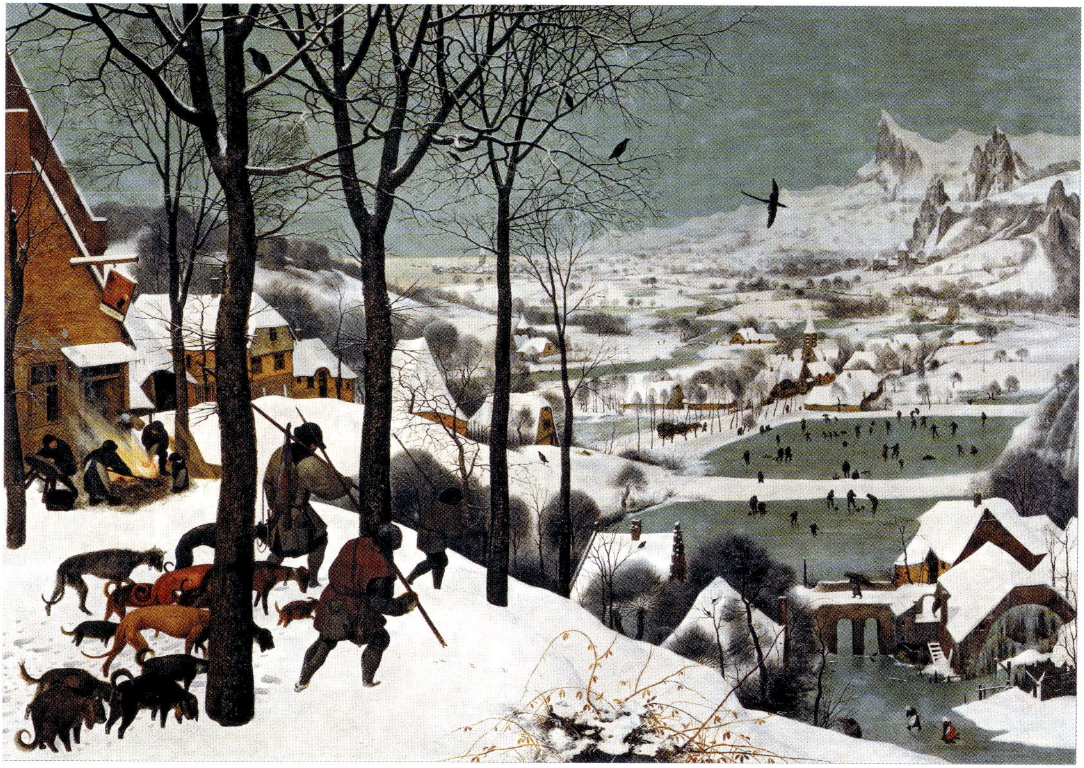

Haymaking, 1565

Oil on oak panel
116.2 × 160.7 cm
Palais Lobkowicz, Prague

Perhaps no other Bruegel painting projects a greater sense of ease than this one. Everything appears to be in perfect harmony beneath a clear sky. People are calmly and peacefully going about their tasks: harvesting the hay, as announced in the title, and picking the beans, cabbages, strawberries and cherries they are carrying home seemingly effortlessly in overly-filled baskets. The picture also follows Bruegel's compositional landscape scheme. From an elevated standpoint we look down across the foreground onto yellow fields where the hay is being raked together and loaded onto carts. Beyond this we see an idyllic village landscape extending behind a typical Bruegel mountain into the blue distance with a river flowing to the sea and the horizon. A mill symbolises the annual cycle of sowing, ripening and harvesting. On the almost monolithic mountain one can make out several huts daringly perched against the rock wall, possibly monks' cells. Behind them, quite small, so far away from the activity, stands a castle, a symbol of the authority that on this lovely warm day plays no (disruptive) role. And nowhere do we see any gallows. The world and humankind are peacefully at one and without a care. In the village at the centre of the picture there is even a traditional archery competition in progress. The three women in the foreground, symbolising the three ages of life, are strolling towards the left with rakes resting on their shoulders in the direction of a mower. They could be a reference to the transiency of youth and beauty, yet the mower has just paused and the young girl who may have made him do so smiles out at the viewer, giving no thought to anything like transiency. It seems as if the cheerful mood has also infected the artist, for he permits himself to make a joke: the woman and two men headed towards the village on the right have balanced their baskets on their heads. The woman carries hers in the normal manner, but the basket on the man in the middle has already settled somewhat and the other man's head has completely disappeared into the basket—or the basket has become his head. One can only hope that he will notice the drop in front of him in time. Given the tensions of Bruegel's time, the painting is almost disturbingly idyllic. Has the painter here taken an artistic break from the horrors and ventured a light-hearted look at a harmonious utopia?

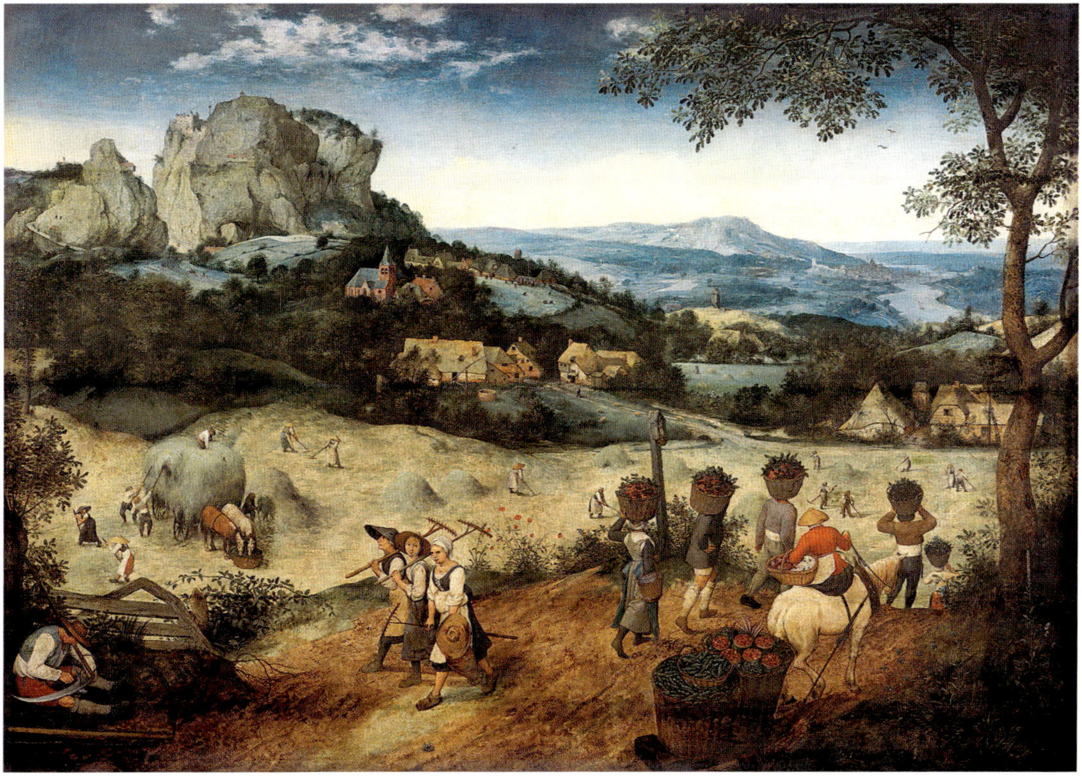

The Gloomy Day, 1565

Oil on oak panel
117.6 × 162.6 cm
Kunsthistorisches Museum, Vienna

In the series of pictures of the seasons this painting represents the months February and March, or early spring, in a typical Bruegel world landscape incorporating everything from the mountains to the sea. The mood is gloomy indeed, due to Bruegel's subtle use of colour, from the dark brown tones in front to the greener shades in the middle distance to the blueish tones towards the horizon. And all this beneath an impressively menacing sky. This mood has not prevented a few souls from having fun: on the right a man armed with waffles is exercising in front of a woman (his wife?), whose child, padded with pillows front and back, wears a paper crown and carries a lantern. In this small grouping Bruegel has conflated Epiphany and Carnival. Oblivious to it, others are busy cutting and bundling willow twigs and one woman is gathering up something from the ground, possibly nuts. The bare trees allow us to see a few of the village buildings. On the far left is the village tavern, in front of which people are making music and dancing, while a man, as so often in Bruegel's pictures, is peeing against the wall. Only a few people are about, which is unsurprising in view of the approaching storm. One villager is still trying to repair the hole in his roof before the violent conditions, already unleashed and raging above the sea, reach the village. The sea is churning, the dikes unable to contain it, so the polders on the right are already inundated. All the ships are casualties of the powerful storm; they have either overturned or suffered damage and are close to sinking. A few people are managing to make it to shore. Far behind the village the tumultuous flood is crashing against the city walls and submerging the beaches. A fortress sits above the city behind which tower the snow-covered peaks of an imposing mountain range. Bruegel presents life's diversity in a single picture. Everything is taking place at once. Some people fail to notice what is about to happen, others don't worry about it and still others appear to be hurrying to take care of the day's chores before catastrophe strikes. In Bruegel death is always present, whether natural or manmade—the gallows is not missing either and crowns the fortress tower. That structure somewhat resembles the Kufstein Fortress, which Bruegel had possibly seen on his journey back from Italy. The only possible sign of hope is the white bird visible high up between the trees. Although it is probably a seagull, it calls to mind the white dove released by Noah to see whether danger has passed.

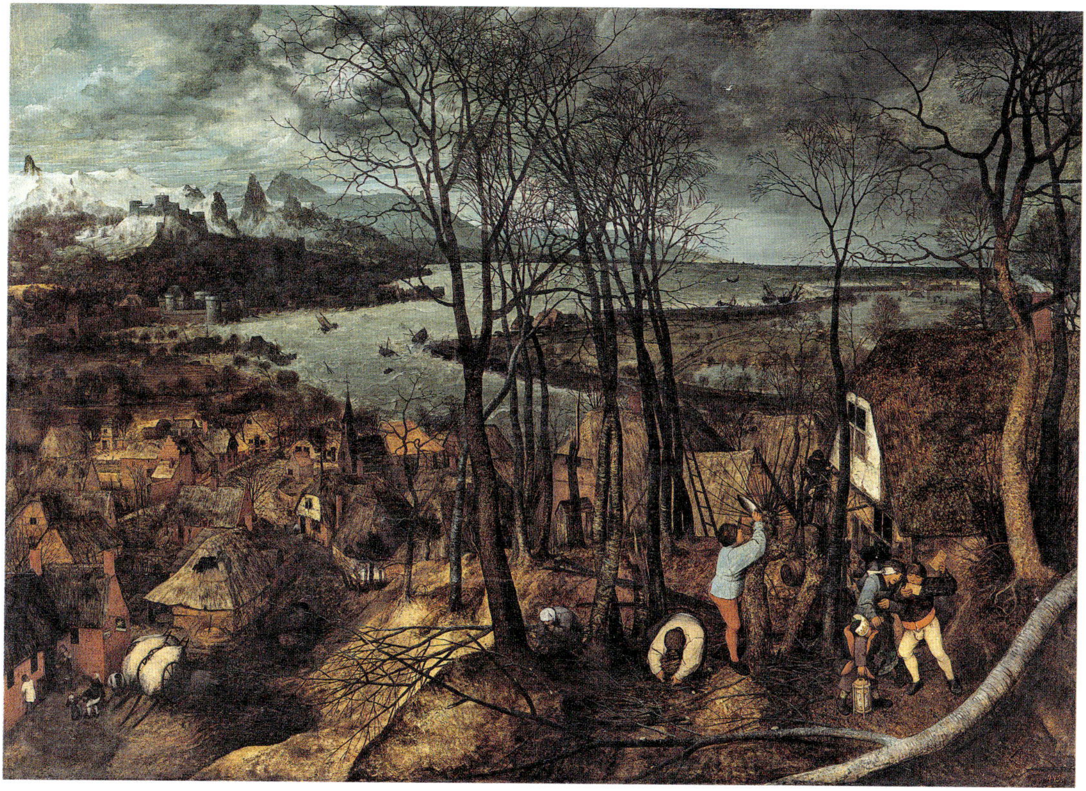

The Massacre of the Innocents, c. 1565–67

Oil on wood
109.2 × 158.1 cm
Royal Collection, Windsor Castle

This work is an example of the rare case that, in some respects, copies (pages 36/37, copy by Pieter Bruegel the Younger) can be more "original" than the original itself. Here the original appears to illustrate "a village plundering", the title given to it in an inventory from 1621. The setting is a snow-covered Netherlandish village square, in the middle of which some thirty mounted soldiers in armour have taken up a position in tight formation. The townspeople are frightened and desperately try to put up a fight. The raiders appear to be plundering all manner of foodstuffs: hams, cheeses, fowls, wild boars, veal and jars of wine. Their brutality seems strangely exaggerated. In the centre of the picture, for example, several soldiers are stabbing at turkeys, a swan and a wild boar (opposite, lower left picture); next to them a woman vehemently refuses to surrender her wine jug and on the left another woman appears to be mourning over a cloth holding ham, ribs and cheese (opposite, lower right picture). Still others hold fabric bundles in their arms. In all these areas the frightening reality of the picture was actually overpainted, for originally, they pictured children being brutally slaughtered. It was in fact not a "village plundering" but the Massacre of the Innocents reported in the gospel (Matthew 2:16), which Bruegel has transferred to a wintry Netherlands in his own time. He seems to be criticising the Spanish occupation forces by way of a Bible story. The red uniforms of the Spanish-Walloon police which could already be seen in *The Way to Calvary* (page 77) and the depictions of soldiers are definitely telling. The Habsburg emperor Rudolf II (1552–1612) was determined to own a Bruegel painting and apparently this was the only one available. But the emperor couldn't stomach the illustrated brutality and had it mitigated by an unknown painter who deburred it by adding victuals, jugs and fabric bundles. But before the picture was "corrected" it had been documented by several contemporaries. Karel van Mander, for example, writes of a "Massacre of the Innocents in which many actual deeds can be seen . . ., how there a whole family begs for the life of a peasant child that one of the murderous mercenaries has snatched and is about to kill". That scene can be seen in the picture's foreground, where instead of the child a calf is about to be slaughtered. Carolus Scribanius, the rector of Antwerp's Jesuit college, wrote about Bruegel's work in his *Städtelob* (*Praise of Cities*) in 1610: "What can one ultimately say once one has seen a small child pierced by a monstrous wound. Oh triumph?" The original horror was also preserved in copies of the painting by Pieter the Younger. The best-known of these are in Vienna and Munich.

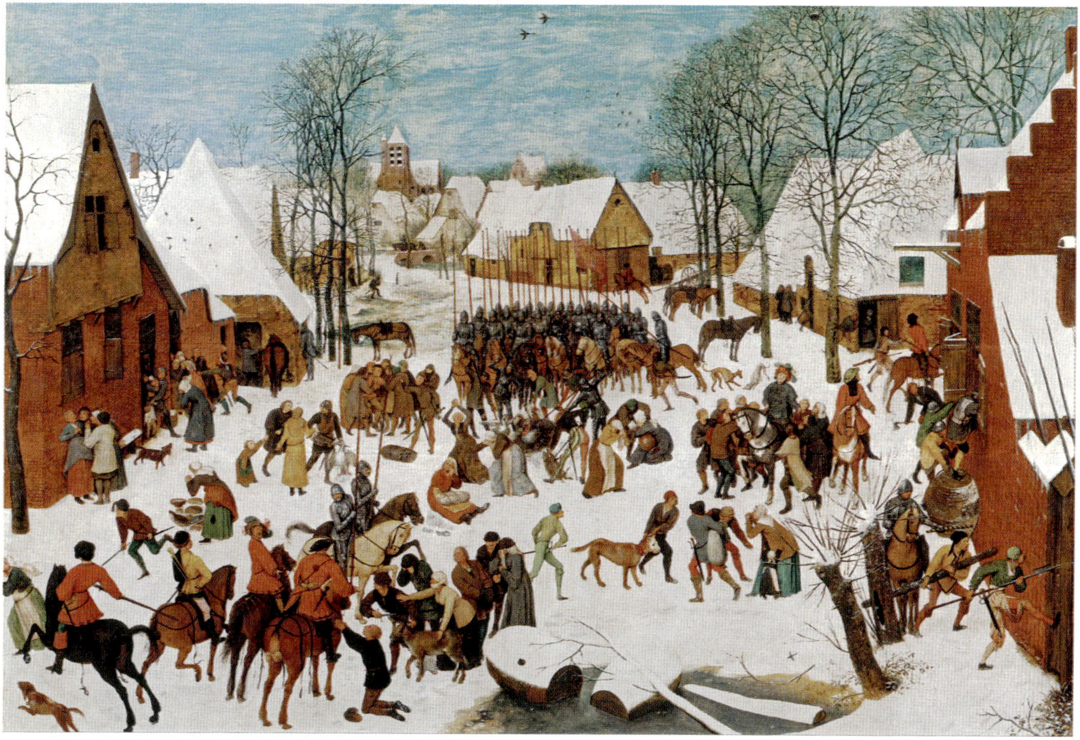

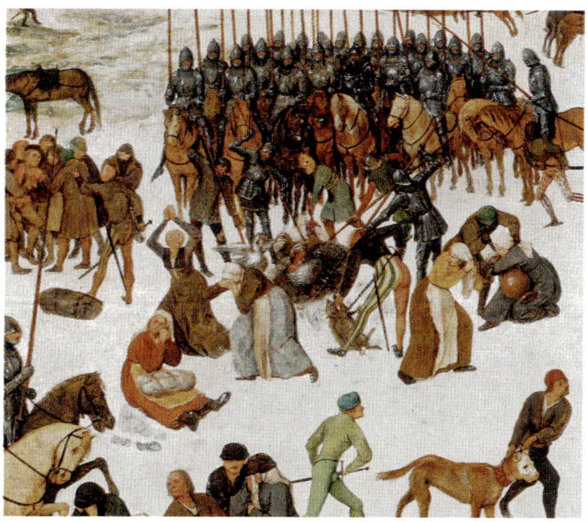

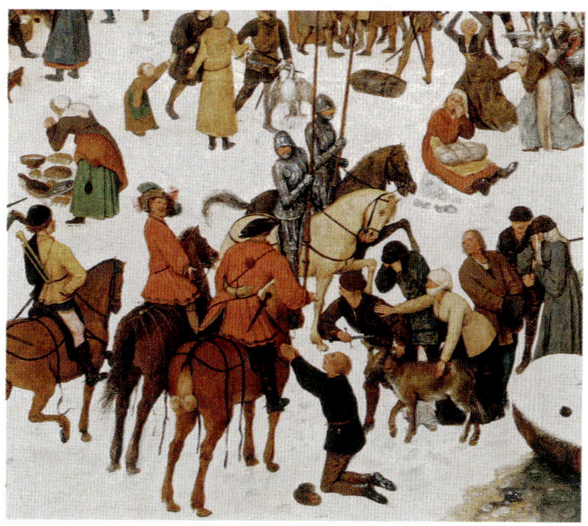

The Census at Bethlehem, 1566

Oil on oak panel
115.5 × 163.5 cm
Musées royaux des Beaux-Arts de Belgique, Brussels

The small village is filled with cheerful, bustling activity: children are playing, sliding on the ice and waging snowball fights by rubbing snow in each other's faces. The grownups are doing grownup chores: all sorts of things are being hauled here and there, people are warming themselves at the fire, a house is under construction and a few locals are permitting themselves a wee drop at an improvised bar in a hollow tree trunk, "The Swan". But the major excitement is in front of the "Green Wreath" tavern, for there the census referenced in the title is taking place. Once again Bruegel has set a biblical event in his own day. This time it is not Caesar Augustus who has commanded it (Luke 2:1–5) but Philipp II; and Mary and Joseph have arrived unremarked by the villagers in order to be counted. It is not only a census but also a tax collection in favour of the Habsburg rulers, as the placard with the double eagle makes clear. This is likely an explicit criticism of conditions at the time. Here again it is unclear who commissioned or purchased the work. The picture already includes events of the coming few weeks, encoded but clearly visible: the search for an inn, the birth of Christ, the Adoration of the Kings, the Flight into Egypt and the Massacre of the Innocents. That Mary and Joseph will find no room in the inn appears to be comprehensible given the crowd. Their search will probably end in the small hut on the right on which a cross already refers to Christ's death and where the Adoration of the Kings will take place, possibly as unnoticed as in Bruegel's painting of it (page 63). Much more significant is the impending massacre: the threat is brewing next to "The Swan". A few lances are leaning against the obviously public building distinguished by a stepped gable and soldiers are emerging from it onto the square. If one relates their appearance to the number of small children in the picture it is evident that something terrible is about to happen. And to make the threat even clearer, from here one's gaze shifts on a diagonal to the slaughter of a pig in the left foreground, which a child watches in horror. It appears as if the child is looking back and forth between the viewer and the dying pig. The narrative's circular movement leads back to Mary seated on a donkey, a foreshadowing of the Flight into Egypt. In the picture's centre stands a single wheel, around which everything is revolving—a recurring symbol of fate in Bruegel's work. Given all the menacing horrors injected into this picture, one almost forgets the sunset, which with the bare treetop alone would produce a wonderful, peaceful painting.

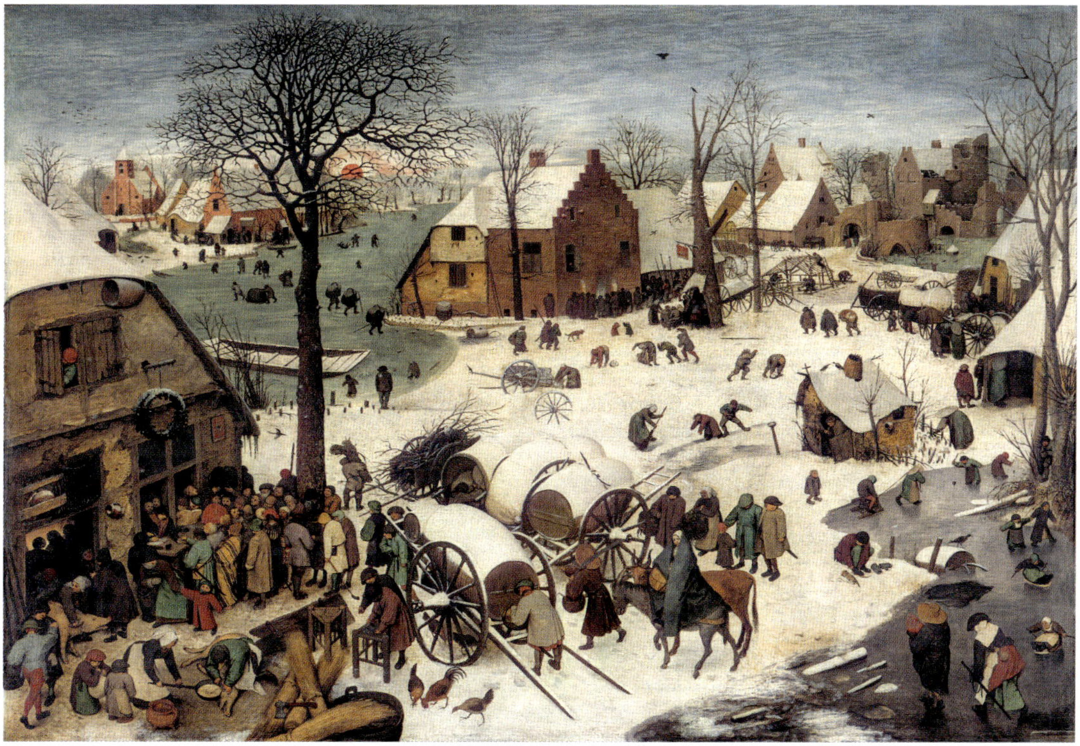

The Sermon of Saint John the Baptist, 1566

Oil on oak panel
95 × 160.5 cm
Szépmüvészeti Muzeum, Budapest

With the onset of the Reformation many thinkers questioned established truths. Luther, Calvin, Sebastian Franck, Erasmus of Rotterdam and many others asked new questions and found new answers and felt called upon to proclaim their truths in public. In sixteenth-century painting this was reflected in a new iconography, one in which John the Baptist played an important role. Increasingly, pictures by Joachim Patinir, Herri met de Bles and Maarten van Heemskerck, for example, pictured him in his function as preacher and baptist. Above all in the Netherlands, where the Reformation and its diverse offshoots were in opposition to the Habsburgs and Spanish foreign rule, the Baptist movement was very strong. In it, children were not baptised shortly after birth, instead adults chose baptism of their own free will. This was a development incompatible with Catholic doctrine. As a result many preachers avoided churches and preached in open fields or in the forest. Such "hedge sermons" were attended by hundreds, sometimes thousands. One can assume that Bruegel at least had such a hedge sermon in mind when painting this work. Here too he related a biblical story to the situation of his own time. And yet as was typical of Bruegel, it was not so much about the event, the sermon itself, as about the circumstances associated with it, namely the great numbers of people who chose to attend such an event. They have come from the distant village with its strikingly large church, following the river, in a bend of which a baptism is taking place, to the edge of a forest. Gathered together are representatives of all faith offshoots and all classes—the diversity Bruegel had come to know in cosmopolitan Antwerp: nobles, burghers, soldiers and peasants, pilgrims and monks. Also Jews, Roma, a turbaned Turk, Chinese and next to them apparently native South Americans, a virtually ecumenical world beyond Christianity. John himself is preaching farther back, pointing in turn to Jesus, wearing a blue robe and surveying the crowd. As so often, the main figures are not the picture's focus, one recognises them only from the attention paid to them by all those around. Almost all, for some are debating or looking for acquaintances in the crowd, still others are paying no attention to the sermon, preferring to read each other's palm. In the upper right stands a silent observer who could possibly be the painter himself. One can read this work not only as a Christian sermon of whatever kind, but as a pictorial expression of a general search for faith that then, as now, played an important, though different, role.

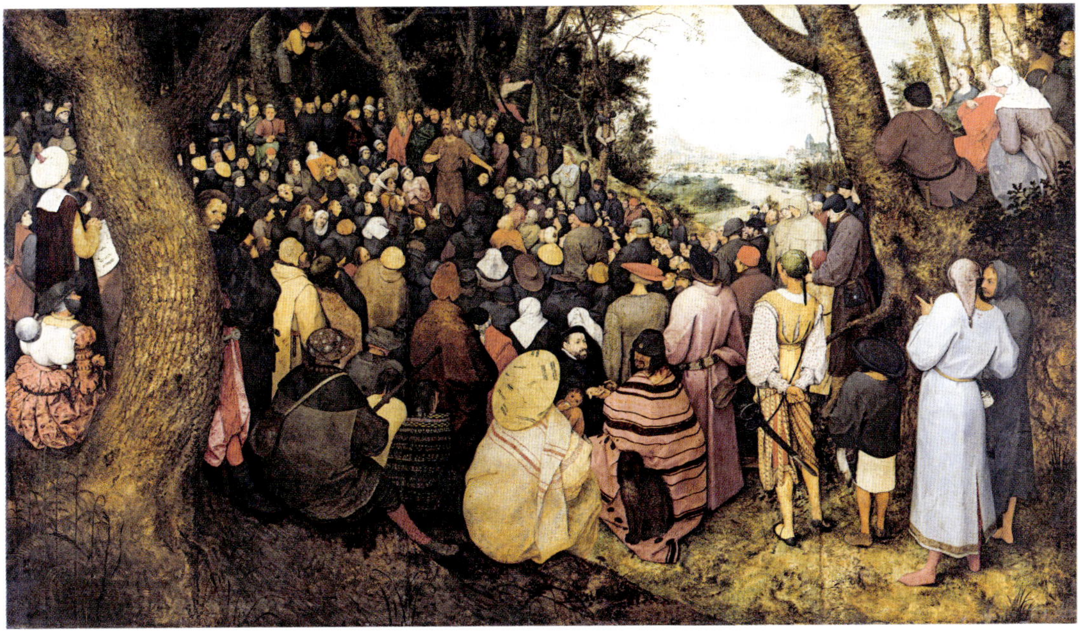

The Wine of Saint Martin's Day, 1566/67

Tempera on canvas
148 × 279.5 cm
Prado, Madrid

One could say that Bruegel's largest work by far is also his newest. It was rediscovered only in 2009/10, purchased by the Prado from a private collection and exhibited for the first time in 2011. The delicate work was not painted in oil on wood, but as a so-called cloth painting with tempera pigments applied directly to a primed canvas. Glazes, or the multiple layers one above the other familiar from oil painting, were hardly possible here. This painting technique was widespread in the fifteenth and sixteen centuries, but owing to its fragility only very few such works have survived. The advantages of the technique were the speed with which the artist could work and the great reduction of expense, the disadvantage its lesser durability. We see roughly a hundred people in the form of a pyramid storming a huge red cask mounted atop some kind of wooden construction. On the right, also filling a pyramidal shape, we see Saint Martin on his horse, the man who according to legend shared his cloak with the beggars. The feast of Saint Martin already fell on 11 November at the time and not only commemorated the saint from Tours but also brought the peasants' fiscal year to a close. On this day farmhands were paid, taxes collected, leases renewed and animals slaughtered so that they did not have to be fed through the winter. A relic of this is the Thanksgiving turkey. And the essential element of this picture, the new wine, or Saint Martin's wine, was served to farmers, beggars and the poor, which traditionally led to debauched carousing. Bruegel's extremely complex pyramid of bodies shows this in all its facets. The people clamour to score as much wine as possible, extending jugs, cups, hats, even shoes. The results are apparent: some men are being sick, hitting each other and dozing, while others, like the man on the left, are lying on the ground in their vomit. The print of a hand on his shirt, an official symbol of Antwerp, identifies him as a beggar who had been given this piece of clothing by the city. Behind him a mother appears to be giving wine to her child, while in front yet another, distracted from drinking wine, fails to notice that a boy is stealing her purse. The subject matter was taken up time and again. Bruegel was possibly inspired by a series of tapestries—the most expensive and exclusive art medium of the time—with motifs from Hieronymus Bosch, one of which pictures Saint Martin's Day. This possibly encouraged Bruegel to produce his own—entirely different—version.

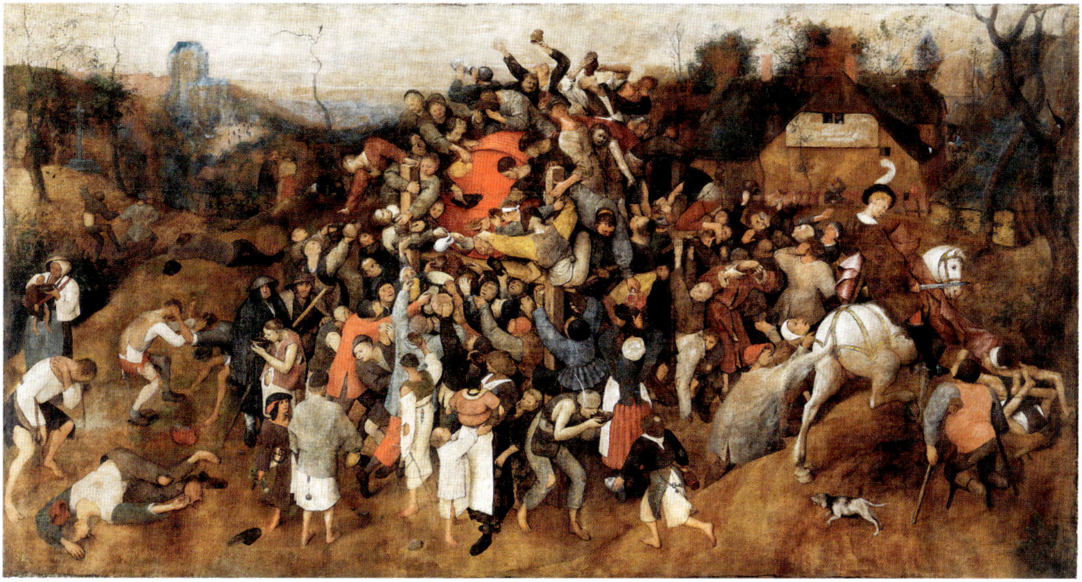

The Land of Cockaigne, 1567

Oil on oak panel
51.5 × 78.3 cm
Alte Pinakothek, Munich

We are witnessing the moment in which a new inhabitant has arrived in the land of Cockaigne. To do so one has to eat through a wall of millet gruel, which the plucky glutton on the right has just managed to do. The land of Cockaigne, the "land of milk and honey", is a fictional country where everything one could wish for is provided in abundance. The ocean is made of milk and every kind of food flies, lies or runs around ready to eat. One only has to dig in, or, if too lazy to do even that, just to open one's mouth. The idea of such a country already existed in antiquity and it appears as an imaginary place in medieval poetry in various versions until the Italian satirist Boccaccio (1313–1375) popularised it as the country Bengodi in his *Decameron* (8th day, 3rd novella). Then people all across Europe talked about such a utopian country with all sorts of freedoms, culinary abundance, open sexuality, social equality and justice. In 1494 the "Scharaffenschiff" (Ship of Plenty) appeared in the 108th chapter of Sebastian Brant's famous *Ship of Fools*—the illustration of which was probably the work of Albrecht Dürer—as a criticism of the feudal system. In 1530 the shoemaker and poet Hans Sachs (1494–1576) published his own version: "a man who wishes to get there has to take on the greatest thing / and eat through a mountain of millet gruel; it is easily three miles thick; / then he is at once / in the land of milk and honey". This is more or less what Bruegel painted: houses roofed with pancakes, fences woven of sausages and a cactus made of flatbread. People everywhere are fascinated by luxurious dishes, of course, which were anything but common in Bruegel's day. The painter also broaches the subject of a world upside down, one already dealt with in his series of prints on virtues and vices. In Cockaigne indolence is as great a virtue as gluttony; industriousness would be a vice, but is logically non-existent. Here a uniformly plump peasant, scholar and knight are lying under a tree. They are splayed like the spokes of a wheel—a motif that turns up in Bruegel time and again, as in *The Way to Calvary* (page 77) or *The Census at Bethlehem* (page 89). They are waiting for the next delicacy from the table built around the tree. Meanwhile a pig is running by with a knife on his back, allowing a slab of bacon to easily be cut out of it and a deliciously roasted goose presents itself on a platter. An egg with a spoon is also on offer but no one can eat any more. One does not get the feeling that Bruegel was here sermonising on the vices of indolence and gluttony; instead, he was simply picturing the popular utopia with much zest and humour.

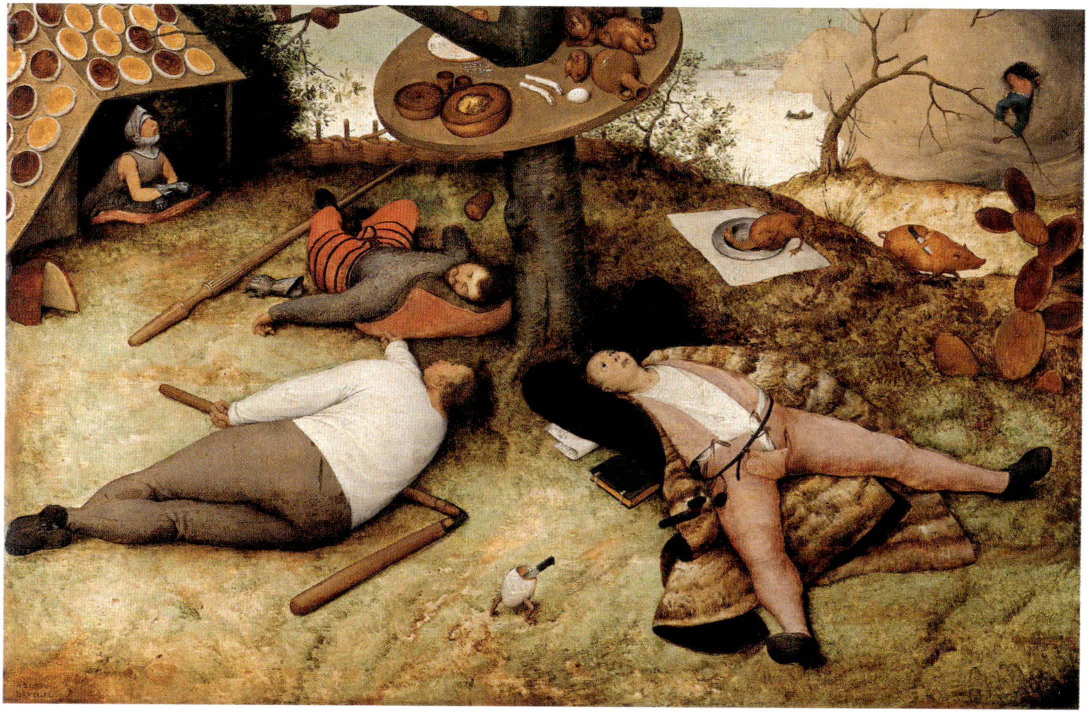

The Conversion of Paul, 1567

Oil on oak panel
108.3 × 156.3 cm
Kunsthistorisches Museum, Vienna

This work has to do with questions surrounding the subject of realisation and insight and the lessons one draws from them. The gospel relates how on the road to Damascus, where he intended to arrest a group of Christians, Saul, a persecutor of the new faith, was blinded by a bright light, fell from his horse and heard a voice saying: "Saul, Saul, why persecutest thou me?" (Acts 9:4). The voice was that of Jesus and Saul realised the error of his ways, had himself baptised and became the preacher and apostle Paul. Bruegel "screens" Saul's fall though it is clearly visible to the crowd around him. His large army is moving up from the coast on the left through a deep mountaintop ravine under a threatening sky. The painting has been trimmed at the top; originally the mountain was even taller. The column appears to have come to a halt, on the right a helmeted soldier is reporting on the difficulties of the road ahead. In all this military movement one almost overlooks the fact that in the centre of the picture Saul, wearing a green robe, the leader of the army after all, has just fallen from his horse. Like the soldiers, most viewers are hardly aware of it. Here Bruegel's approach was totally different from that of previous painters; in the long tradition of works dealing with this subject Saul's fall on being struck by God's ray of light is always the dramatic focus of the picture. In Bruegel, by contrast, the ray of light is also barely visible. How are the soldiers supposed to notice anything? Although we mostly see the figures only from the back, it is clear that the soldiers cannot see a thing; they have drawn their visors so far down over their faces that they are virtually incapable of seeing anything in front of them. In Bruegel non-seeing is generally a sign of non-comprehension or ignorance. It is only Saul himself who appears to have seen the error of his ways. The boy next to him is shielding his eyes with his hand, blinded by the ray of light. All the others continue on their way despite the fierce storm above the mountain heights. As inconspicuous as the "title figure" Saul is, the rider in black, who appears to be the actual commander, is distinctly prominent. The painting was produced in 1567, the year in which the dreaded Duke of Alba moved with his troops into the Netherlands—this man's black clothing resembles Spanish court dress. Alba had massacred great numbers on account of their beliefs; the question of faith had become one of life and death. So it is quite possible that Bruegel was here reinterpreting the Bible story to conform with his own situation. And here again there are ties between the work of art, nearly half a millennium old, and our own day: why do people often have the right insight and yet go off in the wrong direction? And who determines the course of history, the masses or the individual?

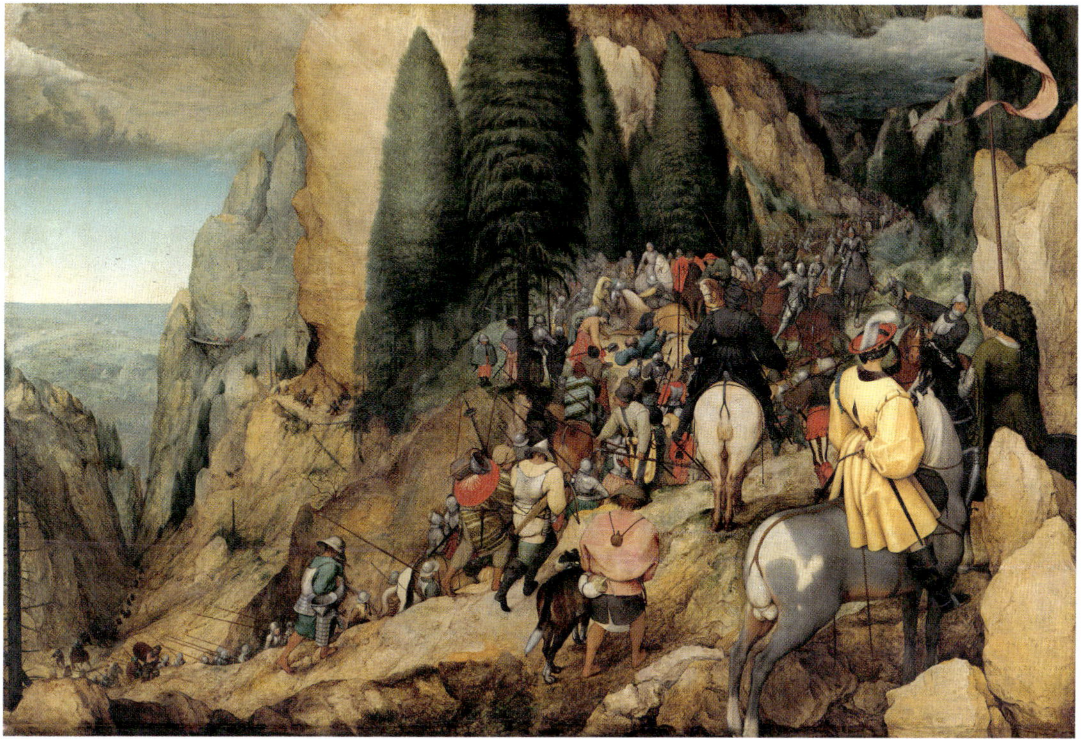

The Peasant Wedding, c. 1567

Oil on oak panel
113.1 × 164.1 cm
Kunsthistorisches Museum, Vienna

With the exception of *The Death of the Virgin* (page 73), Bruegel's most famous painting is his only one set in an interior. There is plenty to eat and drink and music is being provided. The way the artist guides our eye is masterful: we look directly across the boards holding plates filled with mush as well as the man passing them along to the bride. She is slightly tipsy and seated in front of a green wall hanging to which the paper bridal crown has been pinned. To her left are her parents, next to whom a Franciscan monk is debating with the lord of the manor. The latter appears to have arrived unexpectedly as he has been seated on an overturned tub. A second visual axis runs to the left along the table and bench to the door, through which more guests are pressing. The two sightlines cross in the man in an apron carrying plates of mush, whose beribboned red cap identifies him as the bridegroom. He and his helper are serving the guests and have to take care that the table leaves they are using as trays don't suddenly tip to the right. In the foreground a child is licking out the last of a plate of mush and behind him a man is pouring beer out of a large jug into smaller ones. There seems to be a great demand for it. As we now know from infrared photographs many areas of the painting were reworked and desexualised. The front bagpiper's codpiece, for example, now barely visible, was once considerably larger and has been overpainted. It was only one clue, for his pipes pointed to another detail: a couple canoodling up in the hay loft during the festivities. This was also overpainted, thus changing the character of the painting as a whole. In Bible illustration there is a tradition of wedding pictures beginning with the Wedding at Cana (John 2:1–12), at which, at his mother's suggestion, Jesus works his first miracle by turning water into wine. Many artists have successfully tried their hand at it, like Paolo Veronese and Tintoretto—there in the classical style of the Italian Renaissance. Bruegel had spent a good deal of time in Italy but had adopted little of that style: idealised figures filling the picture space and central perspective are not features of his work. He could paint in Renaissance style, of course, but chose to adapt its components for himself and his own purposes. It was his kind of artistic transformation. If one were to imagine nobles celebrating in a ballroom instead of peasants in a barn, one would have a classical Wedding at Cana painted in Renaissance style. That doesn't seem to have interested Bruegel; he "reduced" the biblical subject to a profane one. So one can confidently speak of a miraculous draft of beer.

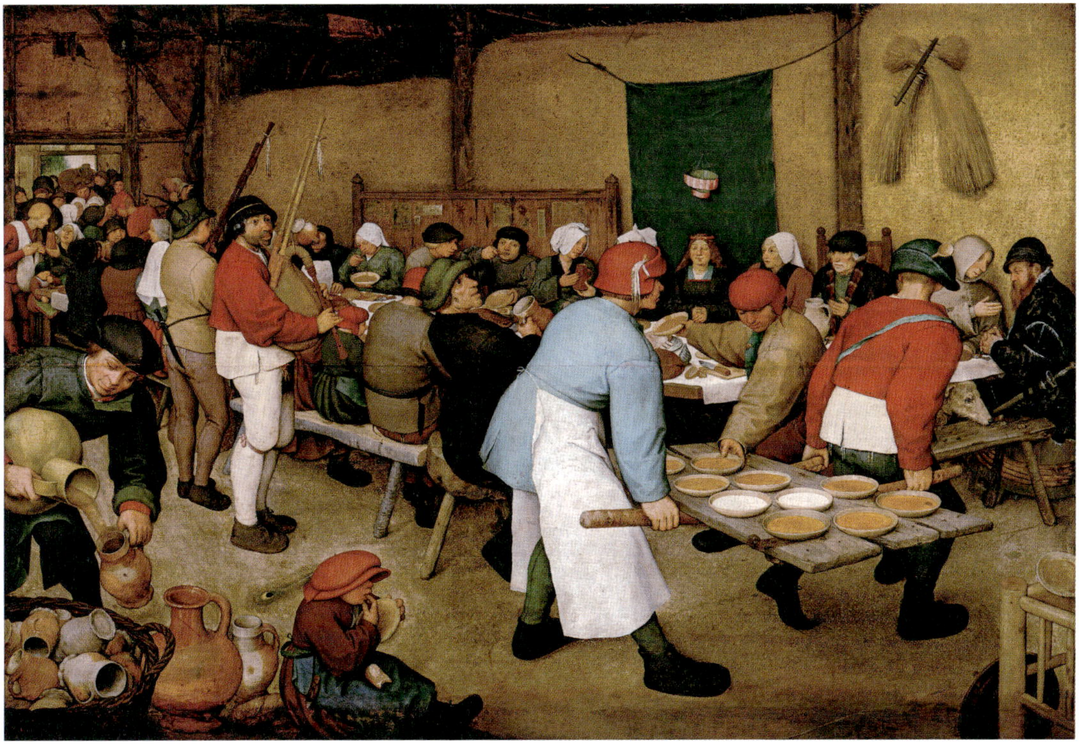

The Peasant Dance, c. 1568

Oil on oak panel
113.5 × 164 cm
Kunsthistorisches Museum, Vienna

It is astonishing how Bruegel could radically change his design principles: unlike world landscapes as in *The Tower of Babel* (page 69) or "busy pictures" like the *Fight Between Carnival and Lent* (page 53), here he moves up close to his figures and observes them at a parish fair as if he was sitting at the next table. His gaze no longer takes in the village and its surroundings as well as the landscape down to the sea, but is blocked a few metres away at the houses and a church. And he no longer offers an exhaustive number of figures but only the few required for his purpose which he characterises individually as needed. Bruegel hurls the viewer into the activity with the couple rushing into the picture from the right. Across the bagpipe player, being bribed to keep playing with beer or wine, the viewer gazes at the table behind him, where a violent debate has broken out, one that may yet end in a brawl. The consequences of the boisterous goings-on here and there that can be ascribed to the eager consumption of alcohol can be seen throughout: a woman is nuzzling up against the man in front of her with his cap over his eyes and behind her a couple are kissing while—as is so often the case—a man is peeing against the wall of the house. Somewhat further away a woman us pulling a man into the house with the large banner and birds all around are screaming from the rooftops about what is about to go on inside. On the village square several couples are dancing, spurred on by a jester and eyed disapprovingly by a somewhat grumpy older man. All the vices appear to be assembled on this village square between the church and the tavern; and the portrait of the Virgin with the Christ child, beneath which hangs a pitcher of fresh flowers, is simply ignored. And because nothing in the painting has been placed there by chance, the broken handle beneath the feet of the foreground couple also has a meaning—lost innocence. But one does not have the impression that Bruegel intended to criticise the goings-on in any way or even denounce them. Art is no moral institution after all. It rather shows the world in its variety, here especially the rural world pictured up close for a change. For this the large-figure Renaissance compositional style—unusually, but clearly employed here—seems ideal. Bruegel avoids any kind of idealisation or condemnation of human activity. He leaves judgement up to his viewers and, depending on the times, social conditions and personal notions of morality, it is always different everywhere.

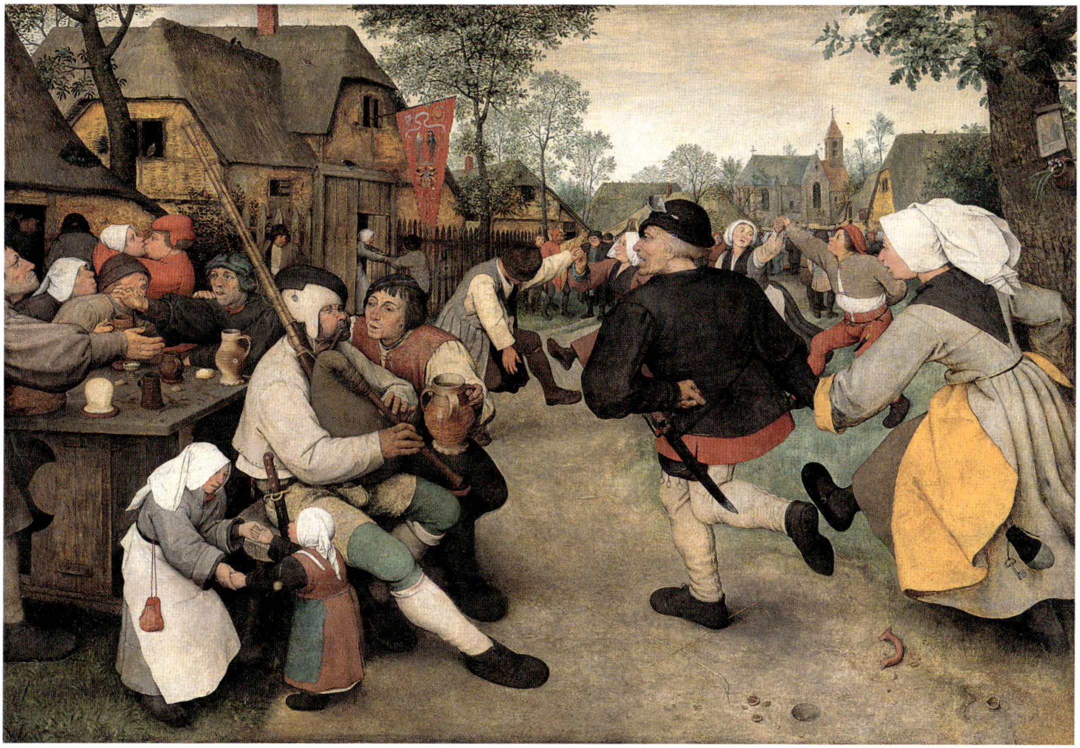

The Beekeepers, c. 1568

Pen and brown ink
20.4 × 30.9 cm
Staatliche Museen zu Berlin, Kupferstichkabinett

Some pictures appeal to us because they seem to withdraw from us. The enigmatic generally has a certain charm and puzzles become interesting only if one doesn't know the solution. It is no different in art. There one is also faced with visual charm and subjected to unexpected emotions. Bruegel's *The Beekeepers* is a case in point: lightly drawn with dense short lines and dots, the drawing confronts us with three figures with unusual head coverings and a fourth who has climbed up a tree. The surroundings seem somehow menacing and surreal—the man on the left is carrying a beehive under his arm and seems to be looking at us without a face—the next one is approaching him slowly and cautiously and the third is about to open a beehive placed upside down. The disconcerting quality comes from the masks that were part of the beekeeper's protective clothing at the time which tend to depersonalise the figures. Did they have the same effect in Bruegel's time? But what are the men doing and why are they wearing protective clothing when there isn't a single bee in sight? And what is the man doing up in the tree? The inscription in the lower left provides little information: "He who knows where the nest is has knowledge; he who robs it has the nest". What nest is meant? The bees' nest? The bee population was an allegory of the Catholic Church, the Christian community, which according to one interpretation was dispersed by the Reformation. So the beekeepers could stand either for a Catholic Church desirous of recapturing its members or for Reform preachers with similar plans of their own. The different powers turn the faithful into subjects. The man in the tree, who has an unobstructed view of the church, recalls the tax collector Zacchaeus, who climbed a tree in order to get a better view of Christ's entry into Jericho (Luke 19:1–10). He is considered a seeker of God but not in the usual institutions. Prominent in the foreground is the big-leafed plant, a mandragora or common mandrake, which because of its anthropomorphic roots had symbolic significance. In a Christian context it was considered salvational and a symbol of man's search for God. All this and still much more—or less—is included in this drawing made during the years of the Spanish Inquisition. A time when it was necessary to hide possible criticism in an image that without a corresponding key—here for the Inquisitors—was a simple genre scene. What Bruegel's intended meaning was can no longer be clarified as we lack the necessary decryption code today.

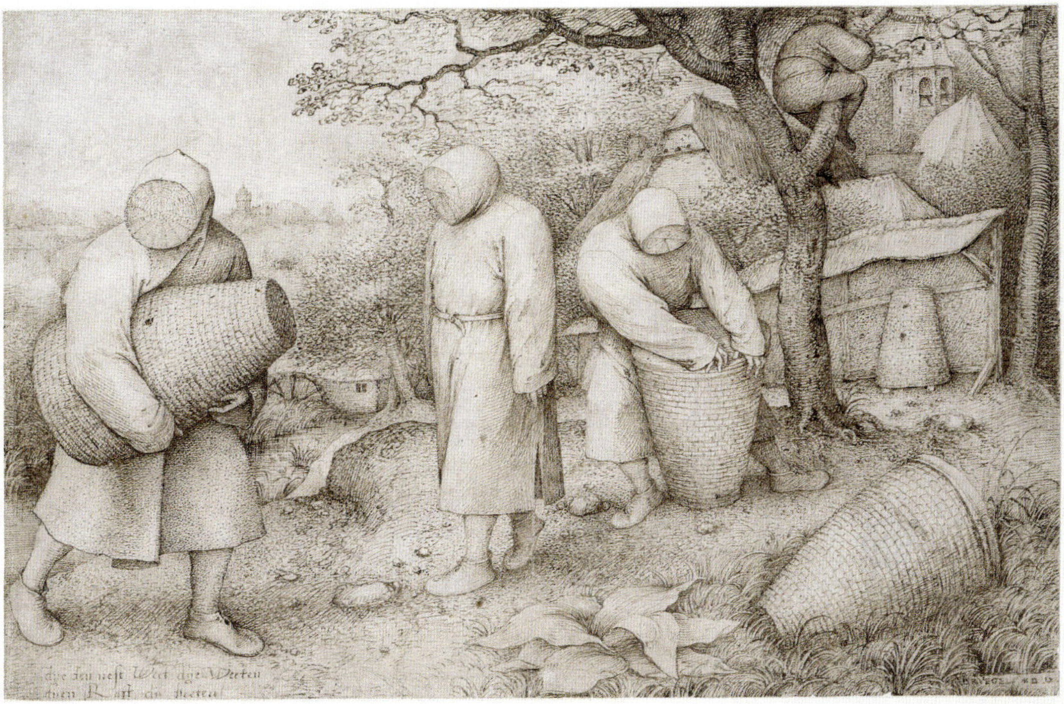

The Blind Leading the Blind, 1568

Tempera on canvas
86 × 154 cm
Museo di Capodimonte, Naples

Six blind men, among them musicians who have performed outside the church, are on their way to the next village. In order to keep together each has placed a hand on the man in front or is holding on to a shared staff. While the last two seem untroubled, the third is already restless, as he has noticed that something in front has gone wrong. The composition is dominated by a descending diagonal leading from the left to the lower right in the direction of the viewer. At the same time it seems as if the men are heading downwards. The man in front has suddenly fallen into the rivulet along with his hurdy-gurdy. The second one has also lost his balance, which Bruegel emphasises by picturing him on only one leg. He will soon fall over as well and the staff he grips with his left hand will in turn cause the third man to stumble, which is clear from his unsteady stance. One senses an acceleration from left to right, a dynamic that will cause all six to fall. Along with this physical dynamic there is also an emotional one: from the anguished cry of the second man to the astonished expression of the man behind him to the insouciance of the blind man at the back, unaware of the goings-on at the front. Bruegel maintains this in that he does not simply picture the blind with closed eyes, as was customary, but instead depicts their various illnesses and injuries so realistically that it triggers debate among eye specialists about their different medical histories. Like *The Wine of Saint Martin's Day* (page 93), the work was painted in tempera on canvas primed with gesso, which has led over the course of time to certain blank spots that can be filled in at least mentally thanks to a copy by Bruegel's son Pieter. On the field in front of the church, for example, several cows, hens and a shepherd, who is calmly leaning on his staff while watching the men's distress, can be seen. As so often in Bruegel the picture is about faith and religion; the source for this one is Christ's denunciation of the Pharisees: "Let them alone: they are blind and leaders of the blind. And if the blind lead the blind, both will fall into the pit" (Matthew 15:14). It could thus be a criticism of the institution of the Church and its priests, one in which the shepherd appears to play an important but unclear role: is he the Good Shepherd or is he indifferent to the suffering of these six blind men—or of all humankind? Or is it aimed at the various preachers roaming about the countryside? Bruegel remains vague in a time of religious and occasionally mortal harassment. One could interpret the shepherd and the landscape with the church either as an idyll or also as simple indifference to mankind.

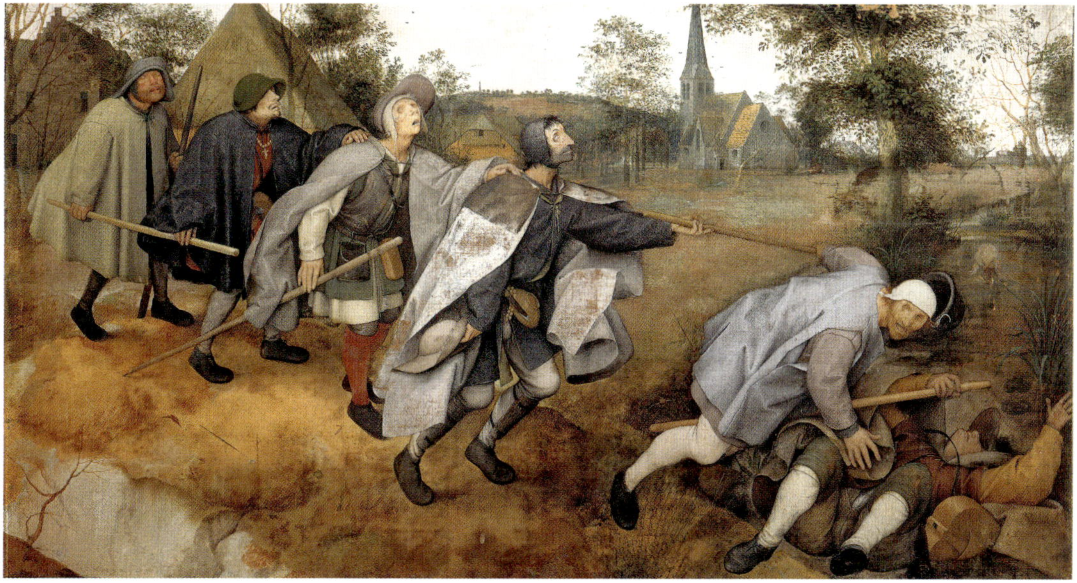

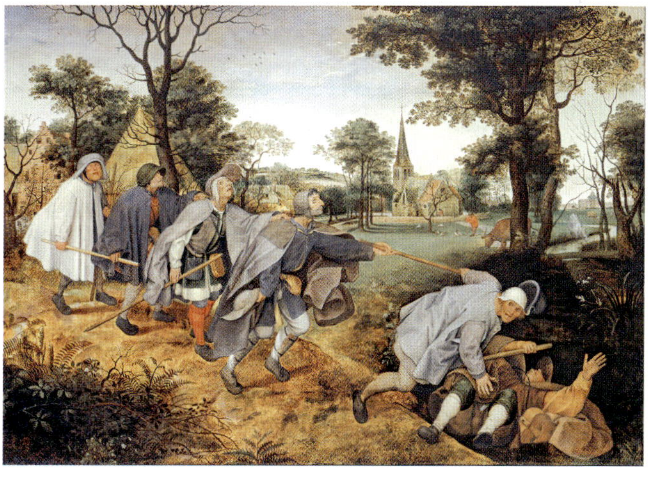

Copy by Pieter Bruegel the Younger,
c. 1610–1620, Louvre, Paris

The Magpie on the Gallows, 1568

Oil on oak panel
45.9 × 50.8 cm
Hessisches Landesmuseum, Darmstadt

If there weren't any gallows in the centre of this picture it would be the purest idyll. It is one of Bruegel's most beautiful landscapes. In the warm afternoon sun people have come to a spot with a view and are dancing to the sound of a bagpipe. In the village below everything seems to be proceeding normally: people are doing their chores, cattle are grazing in the fields, and, on the river, ships are on their way to the city and the ocean beyond. Everything is suggestive of peace—except, of course, for the gallows on which a magpie has perched, a common symbol of gossip and garrulousness. Karl van Mander wrote about Bruegel and this, one of his last pictures, in his *Schilderboeck* of 1604: "In his will he left to his wife a picture with a magpie on the gallows. With the magpie he meant the gossipmongers that he doomed to the gallows". Denunciations and defamations were a grave danger in the heyday of the Inquisition and could promptly send the accused to the gallows. This particular gallows appears to be an unusually shaky structure reminiscent of the complicated perspective constructions of M. C. Escher. Some say that the gallows is dancing and it does seem as if the people below have lost their fear of it—or, as is not uncommon in Bruegel—they couldn't give a proverbial shit about it, as the man in the bushes on the left appears to be doing—a proverb Bruegel also illustrated in his *Netherlandish Proverbs* (page 51). A few metres below the gallows stands a cross at the base of which is a pile of bricks—symbolising a ruined church? And somewhat farther down there is a watermill, its wheel suggestive of the ever-recurring Passion or, if one thinks more positively, the wheel of fortune, alluded to in many of Bruegel's paintings. Scholars consider this to be one of his most puzzling paintings. There is no conclusive interpretation and perhaps none was intended. It seems as if Bruegel, possibly suspecting his early death, once more recapitulated his subject matter and motifs, for even in the depiction of the landscape he harks back to his early pictures in which he frequently cast a panorama-like gaze at virtually ideal landscapes. The migrant crane hovering in the breeze is a symbol of spring and a new beginning. In this picture he could be a counterpart to the magpie and thus a symbol of hope. For perhaps this work was conceived as a utopia, a time when the country would be liberated and the gallows only a painful memory.

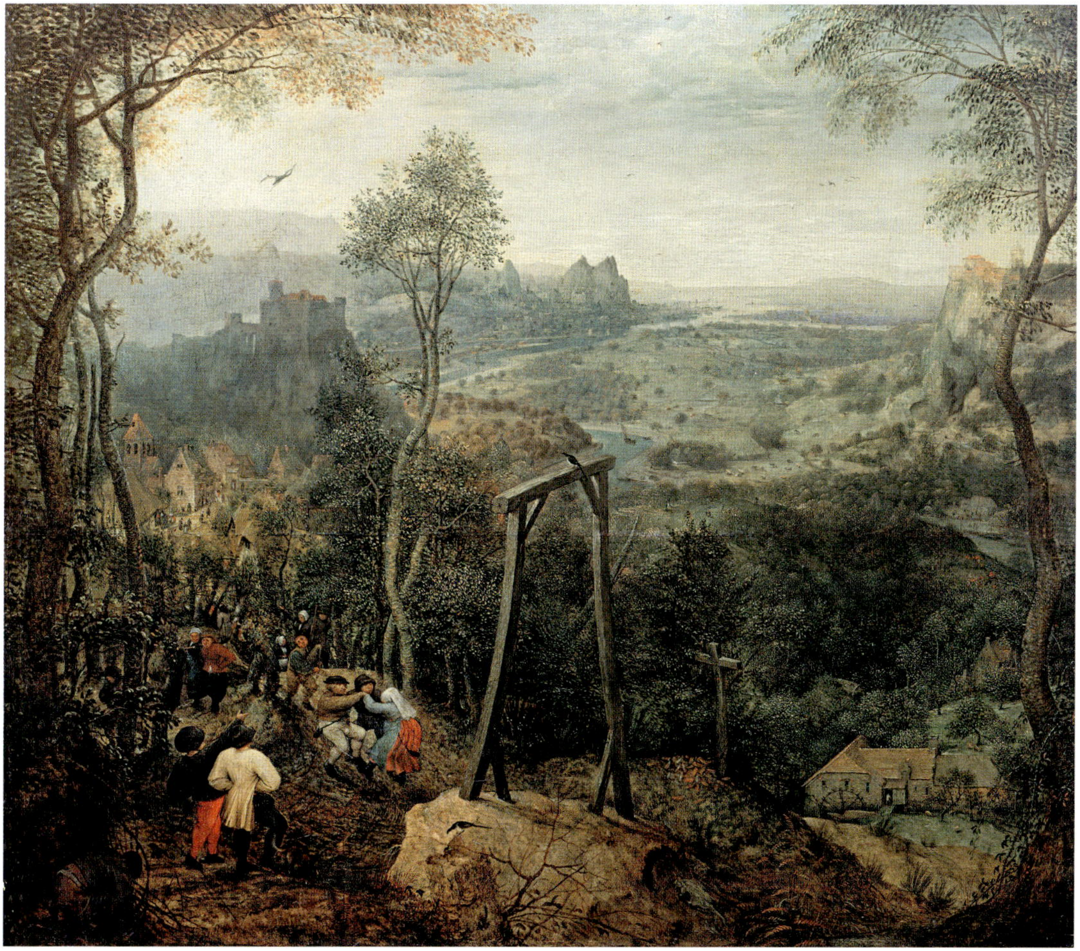

The Battle of the Moneybags and Strongboxes, after 1570

Engraving by Pieter van der Heyden
26.9 × 34.6 cm
Staatliche Museen zu Berlin, Kupferstichkabinett

With an extraordinary combination of fantasy, realism and allegory Bruegel created one of the earliest and at the same time most radical critiques of nascent capitalism. In a virtually limitless battle hybrid creatures composed of men and all manner of money receptacles attack each other: savings boxes, moneybags, barrels and chests are provided with heads, arms and legs. Coins bleed out of their wounds. But who is fighting against whom here and about what? It is a battle about money and money itself is one of the combatants. Everything is fighting everything else. Ordinarily, warring troops are identified by their respective banners, but here there is only one—displaying a grappling hook. The inscription provides a pessimistic take on the scene: "Come on, you savings boxes, barrels and chests, it is all about money and property, this fighting and brawling. Although people tell you otherwise, you don't want to believe it. That is why we feature the hook on our banner that never went astray; people try to disable us, but people wouldn't wage war on each other if there were nothing to steal". The pirate's grappling hook seems a fitting choice as a symbol of capitalism. As a hub of worldwide trade Antwerp had developed into the most important financial centre of the time. All of Europe's banking houses were represented there, experimenting with securities, stocks and other forms of financial speculation. Criticism of this came from multiple directions. Unlike his colleagues, Bruegel did not direct his criticism at the usual suspects such as tax collectors or avaricious merchants but at money itself or emerging capitalism. He had already dealt with avarice in his series on vices in 1558—however this print shows a new dimension. There are no precedents for it; he created an altogether original iconography. Are objects anthropomorphised here or men objectified? The print has no compositional centre, there is no open space, and with the overlappings at the edges the struggle appears to continue ad infinitum: the money war is all that exists. In the bottom right, a dog, the only real creature, is chained to a barrel, which has just been slit open and is also bleeding coins—one of Bruegel's repeated allusions to Diogenes and to his sobriquet "the dog". The barrel to which the dog is chained is filled with money and thus part of what is taking place. So even critics of capitalism are part of the system, or tied to it, and therefore function only within its boundaries. The fact that Bruegel placed his signature precisely here, next to the barrel of Diogenes, indicates his role as critic on the one hand, on the other his recognition of his own involvement. For as an artist he too was dependent on deep-pocketed patrons.

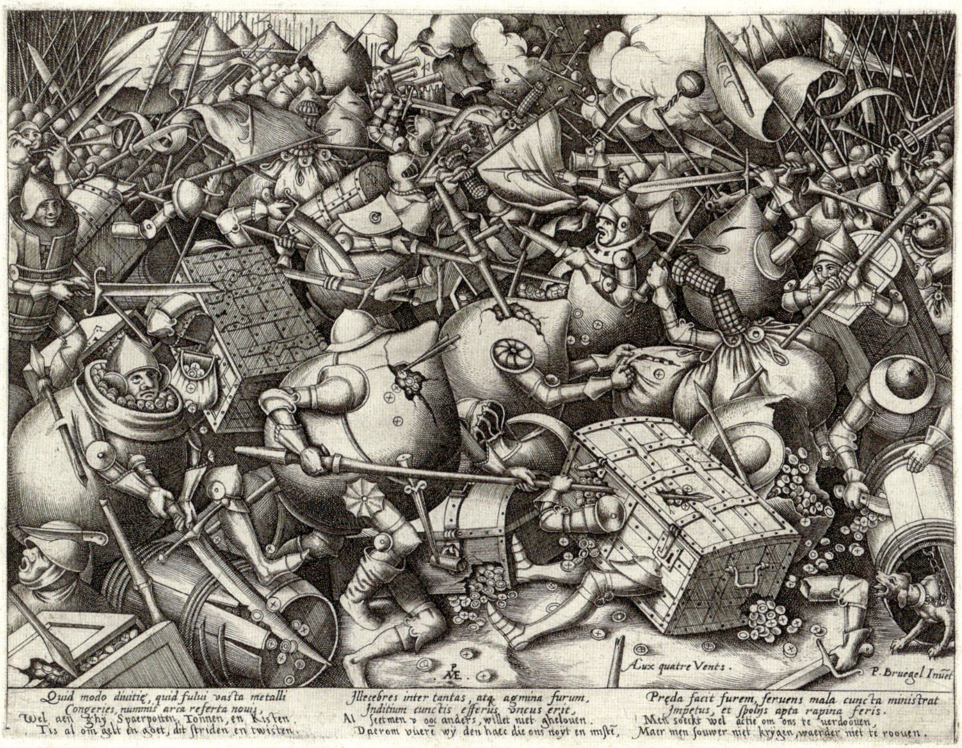
Aux quatre Vents.
P. Bruegel Inuēt
Quid modo diuitię, quid fului vasta metalli
Congeries, nummis arca referta nouis,
Wel aen ghy Spaerpotten, Tonnen, en Kisten.
Tis al om gelt en goet, dit striden en twisten.
Illecebres inter tantas, atq agmina furum,
Inditium cunctis efferus vncus erit,
Al seetmen v ooc anders, willet niet ghelouen.
Daerom vuerē wy den haec die ons noyt en mistē,
Preda facit furem, feruens mala cuncta ministrat
Impetus, et spolijs apta rapina feris.
Men soeckt wel actie om ons te verdoouen,
Maer men souwer niet krygen, waerder niet te roouen.

FURTHER READING

Haag, Sabine (ed.): *Bruegel – Die Hand des Meisters*, ex.cat., Kunsthistorisches Museum Wien, Stuttgart/Vienna, 2018

Hagen, Rainer and Rose-Marie: *Bruegel: Peasants, Fools, and Demons*, Cologne, 2015

Hagen, Rose-Marie: *Bruegel Basic Art: The Complete Paintings*, Cologne, 2000

Meganck, Tine L.: *Pieter Bruegel the Elder: Fall of the Rebel Angels*, Milan, 2018

Müller, Jürgen, and Schauerte, Thomas: *Bruegel: The Complete Paintings*, Cologne, 2020 (45th edition)

Orrock, Amy and Scott, Jennifer: *Bruegel: Defining a Dynasty*, London, 2017

Ritter, Laura, and Peters, Emily (eds.): *Bruegel und seine Zeit*, ex.cat., Albertina, Vienna, Munich/Vienna, 2023

Seipel, Wilfried: *Pieter Bruegel the Elder at the Kunsthistorisches Museum in Vienna*, Vienna, 1997

Sellink, Manfred: *Bruegel in Detail*, New York, 2014

Sellink, Manfred: *Bruegel: The Master*, London, 2018

Vöhringer, Christian: *Masters of Nederlandish Art: Pieter Bruegel*, Cologne, 1999

www.insidebruegel.net

www.bruegel2018.at

PHOTO CREDITS

Artothek: 34, 75 (Fine Art Images – ARTOTHEK)

Bridgeman Images: 8/9, 53, 59, 61, 63, 67, 79, 107; 14 (Reproduced by permission of Chatsworth Settlement Trustees / Bridgeman Images); 36/37 (Christie's Images / Bridgeman Images); 73 (The Bearstead Collection / National Trust Photographic Library / Angelo Hornak / Bridgeman Images); 105 (bottom) (© Erich Lessing / Bridgeman Images)

Detroit Institute of Arts: 33 (City of Detroit Purchase)

mauritius images / piemags / ABTB / Alamy: 15

Staatliche Museen zu Berlin: Cover, 51, 65 (Staatliche Museen zu Berlin, Gemäldegalerie / Christoph Schmidt); 55, 103 (Staatliche Museen zu Berlin, Kupferstichkabinett / Jörg P. Anders); 109 (Staatliche Museen zu Berlin, Kupferstichkabinett / Dietmar Katz)

The Metropolitan Museum of Art, New York: 16/17, 22, 45, 49 (Harris Brisbane Dick Fund, 1926); 21, 47, 57 (Harris Brisbane Dick Fund, 1928); 29 (Rogers Fund, 1919); 43 (Harris Brisbane Dick Fund, 1953)

Wikimedia Commons: Frontispiece, 10, 12, 13, 24, 25, 26/27, 28, 30/31, 32, 35, 38/39, 41, 69, 71, 77, 81, 83, 85, 87, 89, 91, 93, 97, 99, 101, 105 (top); 95 (QS: P170, Q43270) (https://commons.wikimedia.org/wiki/File:Pieter_Bruegel_d._Ä._(1525-1569)_-_Das_Schlaraffenland_-_8940_-_Bavarian_State_Painting_Collections.jpg)

https://creativecommons.org/licenses/by-sa/4.0/legalcode